J. Dunbar

CEO: Chief Evolutionary Officer

Sue Gault
Gus Taccaci

CEO: Chief Evolutionary Officer

Leaders Mapping the Future

August T. Jaccaci
Susan B. Gault

BUTTERWORTH
HEINEMANN

Boston   Oxford   Auckland   Johannesburg   Melbourne   New Delhi

Butterworth–Heinemann supports the efforts of American Forests and the Global ReLeaf program in its campaign for the betterment of trees, forests, and our environment.

Library of Congress Cataloging-in-Publication Data

Jaccaci, August T.
    CEO: chief evolutionary officer : leaders mapping the future /
August T. Jaccaci, Susan B. Gault.
        p.   cm.
    Includes bibliographical references and index.
    ISBN 0-7506-7138-6 (alk. paper)
    1. Chief executive officers.   2. Leadership.   I. Gault, Susan B.
II. Title.
HD38.2.J29   1999
658.4´2—dc21   99-14400
                                                        CIP

British Library Cataloguing-in-Publication Data
A catalogue record for this book is available from the British Library.

The publisher offers special discounts on bulk orders of this book.
For information, please contact:

Manager of Special Sales
Butterworth–Heinemann
225 Wildwood Avenue
Woburn, MA 01801-2041
Tel: 781-904-2500
Fax: 781-904-2620

For information on all Butterworth–Heinemann publications available, contact our World Wide Web home page at: http://www.bh.com

10 9 8 7 6 5 4 3 2 1

Printed in the United States of America

I dedicate this work in appreciation of people who have been very special in my life.

To my mother in gratitude for teaching me to be aware of, respectful of, and in awe of nature and its bountiful gifts.

To my husband, Bill, for strengthening my resolve to write this book and for his continuing support.

To Gus for giving me an exciting new way of framing my life and ongoing evolution in a time of tumultuous and happy change.

To Joanne Spear for living with, encouraging, and contributing to the creation of this book.

I also thank my good friends, Patti Anklam and Mary Utt, for their hopeful guidance and thoughtful review as Gus and I worked to make this book a reality.

Sue

* * *

This work I dedicate to my sons, Tony and Alex, and my nieces, Penny and Sue, for their creative work in the world and for the evolutionary leaders they are becoming.

Because this is a first book long in coming, my gratitude for help runs long and deep.

To Sue Gault, my CEO and C4 coauthor and answer to a down-on-my-knees prayer, for being a writer, editor, graphic artist, photographer, and creative pro in countless ways—strong, sensible, inspiring, and funny—a lifelong best friend.

To John A. Gowan, seeker and finder of the spirit and beauty of nature's patterns, for the diligence and depth of his thinking and for his generous friendship in intellectual and spiritual collaboration.

To Joanne Spear, my life partner and best friend, for loving encouragement and spiritual support of our shared vision when I often lost it; for many ideas that improved the book; and for nobility in pursuing the transformation of health around us and within us.

To my father, Thayer, for his artistic creativity; my mother, Helen, for her social creativity; my sister, Gail, for her courageous and patient generosity.

To my mentors who have "gone yonder" for their guidance: Saint Francis, Thomas Jefferson, Bucky Fuller, Derald Langham, Ben Bentov, Stuart Dodd, Margaret Mead, John C. Gowan, Zee Persons, and Helen and Thayer.

To my friends at CPSI for their creative help, encouragement, and evolutionary vision: Sid Parnes, Bill Shepard, Don and Ruth Ann Ferris, Bill Sturner, Marilyn Norris, Bee Bleedorn, John Hornecker, Lillian Maresch, Rosalie Deerheart, Ken Cox, Judy Jones, Lois Pinkowski, Cesar Diaz-Carrera, Michael Snyder, Nancy Wilson, Nancy P. Wilson, Larry Robinson, and all the other wonderful doers and shakers I have met yearly for more than a quarter of a century.

To my friend-evolutionaries who have helped me with their lives to define that role: Rendle Leatham, Mary Baker, Roger Brown, Ann Brainerd, Michael Ray, Eric Vogt, Dick Wilson, Laurie McCammon, Annie Campbell, Hunter Ingalls, Ian Baldwin, Ken Baskin, Jim Mitchell, Benny and Denise Reehl, Dan Winter, Barbara Hubbard, George Land, Tony Judge, Hunt Barclay, Baron and Baroness Killi and Edme Di Pauli, Sir George Trevelyan, Marilyn Ferguson, Seth Itzkan, Peter and Pam Coakley, Fred Glimp, Twylah Nitsch, Jean Rindge, Ken Hamilton, Laurie Cartier, Maryiln and James Rockefeller, Tim Wirth, Ron Klein, Jim Webber, George Lichte, Curt Lindberg, and Dirk and Ragnhild Bornhorst.

And finally, to our group of social C4 pioneers for their love and courage and conscious, creative, collaborative, compassionate community: Alex Jaccaci, Maureen Burford, Maryanna Bock, Chris Holton-Jablonski, Jeremy Youst, Helaine Iris, and Carol Mahoney.

Gus

Contents

Illustrations xi
Foreword by Ken Baskin xiii
Preface xv
The METAMATRIX® xviii
Process-Pattern of This Book xx

Part I Evolution Is the Only Business 1

Chapter 1 Era of Evolution (*Gus*) 3
Conscious Evolution 4
Acceleration of Evolution 4
The Evolutionary 5
Chief Evolutionary Officer 6

Chapter 2 Nature's Patterns of Success (*Sue*) 11
Pattern and Predictability in General Periodicity 12
Transformative Growth 14
Natural Order as a Thinking Tool 15
The METAMATRIX® Map and Natural Order 16
Four-Column Overview Thinking 19
Potential for Infinite Growth 20
Applications of the METAMATRIX® 20

Chapter 3 Discovering a Pattern of General Periodicity (*Gus*) 23
Buckminster Fuller 26
Margaret Mead 29

Barbara Hubbard   31
Creations at the Creative Problem Solving institute   32
Discovering a Pattern   33

Chapter 4   Converging Paths (*Sue*)   **39**
Getting Started   39
Technical Writing   39
The Path to Leadership   40
What Next? The Beginnings of Transformation   44
Chief Evolutionary Officers in Business   45
Values of a Chief Evolutionary Officer   46
Conscious Evolution   46
Creativity   47
Collaboration   47
Compassion   48
Visionary Idealism   48
Definition of Vision   49
Examples of Past Visionary Leaders   50
Characterization of the Chief Evolutionary Officer   50

Chapter 5   Creating the METAMATRIX® (*Gus*)   **53**
Creation of the METAMATRIX®   53
The Map of Human Evolution   60
Gathering Stage of the Species   62
Repeating Stage of the Species   63

Chapter 6   Evolutionary Bridge Building (*Sue*)   **67**
Evolutionary Context for Domain Mapping   68
Business Leading Evolution   70
Good Business Equation   71
Power of Prediction   72

Part II   Life Is the Only Customer   **75**

Chapter 7   Creating the METAMATRIX®
Domain Map (*Gus*)   **77**
Domain Mapping   78
Health and Nutrition: The First Domain   80

Chapter 8   Domain Mapping (*Sue*)   **83**
Dynamics of the Information Age   85
Differentiating Products from Services   87

Chapter 9   How to Map a Domain (*Sue*)   **93**
The Generic Domain Map   93
Questions on the Generic Domain Map   95

Chapter 10   Sample Domain Map (*Sue*)   **103**
New Creations   106
Managing Successful Creations   108
Food Domain Services   109
Creating Ideal Intention   110

Chapter 11   Creating Conscious Renaissance:
R$_t$ Time (*Gus*)   **115**
Time of Rebirth   115
Time of Questioning   116
A Time for Social Architecture   118

Part III   Community Is the Only Profit   125
Chapter 12   Community: Evolution's Vessel (*Gus*)   127
Community Redefined   128
Web of Life   129
Evolving Evolution   131
Beyond Darwinism   131
Future Human Evolution   133
Pioneering C4 Communities (S$_g$)   136
Community Contexts (S$_r$)   136
Global C4 Value News (S$_s$)   137
Peace and Health in All Relations (S$_t$)   137

Chapter 13   Exploring C4 Community (*Sue*)   **139**
Stories of C4 Communities   140
Salvaging Bluebeard's Ship   140
Community Health Insurance   141
Nucor Steel   141

Clearing Overgrowth with Sheep 142
Land institute in Kansas 143
Creating C4 Community 144
Dynamics of Sharing 144
Integration in Summary 147
Transformative Growth 148
Illustrative Maps 149
C4 Values 150
Ideal Intentions 151
Synthesis in Summary 151
Farewell 153

Chapter 14 Call for a New Story of the Cosmos (*Gus*) 155
Cosmology: Creating Our Own Story 155
Conscious Cosmology 156
Creative Cosmology 157
Collaborative Cosmology 157
Compassionate Cosmology 157
Social Architecture of C4 Community 157
Map of Social Architecture 159
Map of Human Learning 161
Individuals and Species as Reciprocal Learners 166

Part IV   Love Is the Only Future 169
Chapter 15   The Higher-Order Unity of Love (*Gus*) 171
Convergence in Transformation 172
Call for the Cosmology of Love 176

Bibliography 181

Index 187

Illustrations

FIGURES

Figure P–1	METAMATRIX® Map	xviii
Figure 2–1	METAMATRIX® Map	17
Figure 2–2	Fractal Pattern of Fern Frond	18
Figure 3–1	Fuller's Dymaxion Map	27
Figure 4–1	METAMATRIX® Map of Career to Date	42
Figure 5–1	METAMATRIX® Map in Sixteen Stages	55
Figure 5–2	Proportions of the Golden Rectangle	57
Figure 5–3	Rectangle Divided into Square and New Golden Rectangle	58
Figure 5–4	Golden Rectangle with Spiral	58
Figure 5–5	METAMATRIX® in Golden Rectangle	59
Figure 5–6	Map of Past and Present Human Evolution	61
Figure 6–1	Overview of Food Domain Map	68
Figure 6–2	Domain Map Set in Map of Human Evolution	69
Figure 7–1	Original Domain Map of the Food Industry	80
Figure 7–2	Completed Domain Map of the Food Industry	81
Figure 8–1	Overview of Domain Map	84
Figure 9–1	Generic Domain Map with Questions	94
Figure 9–2	Transformation into New Domains	100
Figure 9–3	Domain Map Transform Stage	102
Figure 10–1	Domain Map with Food Industry Questions	104
Figure 10–2	Sample Domain Map of the Food Industry	105
Figure 12–1	Sharing Stage of Human Evolution	135
Figure 13–1	Summary Map of Our Book	148

Figure 14–1   Map of Social Architecture   160
Figure 14–2   Map of Human Learning   163
Figure 15–1   Four-Column Map of Human Evolution   173
Figure 15–2   Four-Column Map of Human Learning   174
Figure 15–3   Four-Column Map of Social Architecture   175

TABLES

Table 2–1   Examples of Four-Column Thinking   19
Table 3–1   Organization of Nature   35
Table 6–1   Gather, Repeat, Share, and Transform Progressions   73
Table 8–1   Four Columns of Domain Mapping   86

Foreword

CEO: Chief Evolutionary Officer is a perfect title, capturing an idea so powerful that it's self-evident . . . as soon as someone else points it out. I'd been writing for years about organizations operating as if they were living things, and I still wrestled with the question of how anyone could *lead* such self-organizing entities. And here Gus Jaccaci and Susan Gault had pinned it to the page by shifting one word. Such organizations, they suggest, don't need leaders who identify and execute direction, as if they were driving a corporate machine. Rather, they need leaders who will guide organizational evolution—chief *evolutionary* officers, *not* chief executive officers.

I should have expected as much from Gus Jaccaci. I'd met him on Halloween 1993, when I first heard him explain the METAMATRIX®— the tool for understanding the future that he and Sue Gault introduce in *Chief Evolutionary Officer*—to a group of friends. Back then, he claimed that the METAMATRIX® could map any system that develops through a cycle of growth and transformation, and I wondered, but not for long, how he could be arrogant enough to make that claim.

As Jaccaci talked, his eyes sparkled and danced, luring us into the world he was building. His voice welcomed and comforted, creating a safe space around us. At the same time, his body was constant motion, as if he were walking the verbal journey on which he led us. At his best, he could disarm skeptical listeners, convincing them to drop resistance with a single, expertly pointed question. Jaccaci was, and is, a teacher's teacher.

In the years since, I've seen Jaccaci use the METAMATRIX® to map growth cycles as different as human history and personal psychological development. I've watched John Gowan—whose ideas helped develop it—use the METAMATRIX® to map the two extremes of such transformational systems—subatomic structure and the cosmos. I've used it myself to map corporate transformation.

In every case, this tool yielded powerful insights into the emerging future.

In *Chief Evolutionary Officer*, Jaccaci and Gault take leaders through a step-by-step demonstration of how they can use the METAMATRIX® to see the emerging future. It is clear that the emerging future will be very different from what we know today. As a result, one critical challenge for leaders who would guide their organizations' evolution into the 21st century is to gain an insight into what that future will be.

What the METAMATRIX® teaches them is that, as in all transformational systems, organizational growth is unceasing, but the nature of that growth does shift. Today, we stand at the transition between two fundamentally different types of change.

In Chapter 5, Jaccaci and Gault explain that transition, from the "Repeat" stage of growth, in which systems grow by repeating what's worked for them, to the "Share" stage, in which they grow by leveraging differences within the system. After all, the 20th century was an era of mass production, when everyone, from automakers to insurance providers and even educators, sought to turn out the same product or service over and over, to repeat whatever worked on a mass level. In contrast, the Share stage we're now entering will be a time of mass customization, in which business people will profit from meeting a range of very different needs in their markets.

For corporate leaders, the transition from Repeat to Share suggests that business success will depend on moving from standard products and services to those that enable people to enhance their personal lifestyle choices. If you're not sure that this transition is already under way, think about the corporate movement from one-package-fits-all benefit plans to cafeteria-style benefits that recognize the very different needs of single employees and those with young families.

With this insight, chief evolutionary officers can guide their organizations into new ways of thinking about their markets. The food industry, for example (Chapter 10), is moving from mass food production to giving people the choice of nutrition styles that will help them focus on physical fitness, spiritual awareness, or other lifestyle objectives. Markets for goods and services as different as entertainment, furniture or clothing making, and even education or electric utilities, are shifting similarly.

Moreover, Jaccaci and Gault make today's market shifts seem less intimidating, if no less difficult, by demonstrating that they reflect a universal pattern, rather than random changes that defy understanding.

As if all this weren't enough, *Chief Evolutionary Officer* has one last gift to offer us. In a time of crisis, when local TV evening news might more accurately be called the nightly crisis count, Jaccaci and Gault explain that we are not merely in crisis. Rather, the breakdown of community and old values marks the inevitable birthing pains of any system evolving from one stage of growth to another.

For that reason, they urge all of us to be our own chief evolutionary officers and cultivate, throughout our lives, the chief evolutionary officer's values, the "four Cs" of *conscious evolution, creativity, collaboration,* and *compassion.* In this way, we can all contribute to the era being born, an era that will witness the rebirth of community and the recognition that we can use our enormous wealth-producing capacities for the benefit of everyone in our communities . . . and on the planet.

Ken Baskin
Author, *Corporate DNA: Learning from Life*
Senior Partner, Life Design Partners

Preface

This is a book about human evolutionary potential and how to envision and act on that potential. *CEO: Chief Evolutionary Officer* explains how to use natural order to predict and design an ideal future. That is, we use natural order as the basis for conscious evolution.

Taking the broadest and most encompassing picture is important to us. That picture sets the stage for evoking and enhancing the evolutionary best in all of us. To that end, we use human evolution, past, present, and future, as the framework for the greatest individual, communal, and planetary potential.

In coauthoring this book, we learned what it means to express our own potential. As individuals, we are more complementary than similar. Gus can be described as theoretical, transcendent, and an idealist. Sue, on the other hand, is practical, immanent, and a realist. When combined, our thoughts and viewpoints gain strength and usefulness. Together we form a union of differences that can be visionary, constructive, evocative, and creative. It is the union of our potential that we wanted to bring to this book.

To present our combined strengths, we designed a two-threaded approach to the book. Gus wrote the theoretical chapters. Sue interwove Gus's chapters with her chapters, which have a practical focus. We liken the approach to a two-member track team running a relay race: Members contribute their individual best and work toward a common goal, passing a baton as proof of their coordinated effort. The Table of Contents of this book specifies which one of us is carrying the baton at the moment so that the reader can know who is speaking in addition to what is spoken. In this way, for example, Gus can tell his story about the thinking and experiences that led to his discovery and creation of the METAMATRIX® as a nature-based thinking tool, and Sue can bring her business-based background to bear in the application of the METAMATRIX®.

THE METAMATRIX®

The METAMATRIX® is a visual thinking map based in the natural process-pattern of transformational growth. This map is the basis for both the content and the structure of *CEO: Chief Evolutionary Officer*. It shows, in whatever level of detail or abstraction you like, the natural evolution of anything that grows, for example, groups, companies, or beaver colonies. Each cycle of this natural growth process-pattern comprises four different dynamic stages: gathering, repeating, sharing, and transforming. We represent each four-stage cycle in a METAMATRIX® map in Figure P–1.

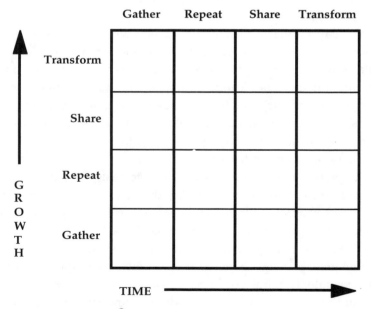

Figure P–1   *METAMATRIX® Map*

Evolutionary growth and change are a natural process with a pattern of sequential stages. That order is why we can represent evolutionary growth in the METAMATRIX®. The three stages of gathering, repeating, and sharing lead to the fourth stage of transformation and the start of another new growth cycle. Once one cycle is completed, another cycle of the same four stages can begin.

We show the primary stages in vertical columns and their identical substages in horizontal rows. The combination of the substages within larger stages and the ability to grow to a new four-stage cycle when the previous one is complete makes the METAMATRIX® a fractal structure. Natural design often incorporates such fractal structures in which self-similar parts recur in larger and larger sizes, just as the veins in a leaf reflect the larger branching structure of a tree.

Each stage has its own unique and dominant dynamic that guides successful development within that stage. We call these sequential stages gathering, repeating, sharing, and transforming (GRST) because these terms capture the essential dynamic of their respective stages. The stages are necessarily GRST sequential, like the stages of growth in a human life. In the body of this book, we examine these stages in greater detail. For now, suffice it to say that because we know their creative dynamics and sequence, we all can predict general growth and evolution.

Prediction gives all of us the ability to envision and create an ideal future. Knowing the sequence of stages and the dominant dynamic of each lets us use the stages to support the creation of our desired future. Because we can determine our current stage, we can look to future stages and, by applying the dominant dynamic for each stage, help to form its natural, successful unfolding, just as we can look at infants and foresee their future growth stages.

In this book, we use the METAMATRIX® in a variety of ways. The following three applications of the METAMATRIX® support the main themes of this book and recur throughout:

- The map of human evolution is an application that provides the broadest possible context and greatest growth potential for the themes of this book.
- Domain mapping tells leaders of all kinds how to envision and plan for the successful growth of their enterprises.
- The social architecture map and the map of learning help chief evolutionary officers create intentional evolutionary communities.

Throughout all of the METAMATRIX® maps, the natural growth process-pattern of gathering, repeating, sharing, and transforming provides a unifying dynamic and consistent framework.

PROCESS-PATTERN OF THIS BOOK

Following the four stages of GRST, we have written this book in four parts. Each part is titled with an ideal intention that expresses our greatest evolutionary hope for humanity and sets the theme for the part:

Part I, Evolution Is the Only Business, is the gathering part of the book. We introduce both ourselves and the philosophies on which the book stands. Gus sets the stage for an era of evolution and explains his creation of the METAMATRIX® and its application in the map of human evolution and domain mapping. Sue grounds the philosophies in natural order and talks about her business background and subsequent interest in METAMATRIX® applications.

Part II, Life Is the Only Customer, is the repeating part of the book. We examine the practical matter of growing enterprises, including for-profit businesses, using domain mapping. As enterprises evolve from the repeating stage to the sharing stage, they also evolve from products to services. Service to life, the only real customer, becomes a central intention.

Part III, Community Is the Only Profit, is the sharing part of the book. We present the subject of community and its great potential for human sharing and fulfillment. We define conscious, creative, collaborative, and compassionate community (C4 community). We look at the human evolution, social architecture, and human learning that can make healthy community the only profit.

Part IV, Love Is the Only Future, is the transforming part of the book. We propose a higher-order unity of global culture and human species learning and evolution. The wisdom of the universe is given to humanity. Our business becomes the creation of a cosmology of love that unifies the planetary community of all life into an enlightened state of being.

Part I

Evolution Is the Only Business

This is the first time in the history of our species that we are all awakening to the call to take responsibility for our own healthy human evolution. Our purpose in writing this book is to help you transform this critical call into a creative action plan in your life and work. We honor your willingness to take creative leadership initiatives. The creators of new domains of human endeavor are the architects of emerging culture, the visionary voices of evolution. As you rise to this call, we will show you that healthy evolution not only is good business but also is the only business.

1

Era of Evolution

For hundreds of years, humanity has seen revolutions in the life of our species—political, economic, scientific, artistic, spiritual, and in all other domains of endeavor. These revolutions of radical, often violent, change have been led by revolutionaries like Thomas Jefferson, Karl Marx, Albert Einstein, Pablo Picasso, and Martin Luther. These revolutionaries have been passionate, visionary actors on the stage of human creation, freedom, and wisdom. People live as daily students of these revolutionaries and often as the beneficiaries of their gifts. Yet the day of the revolutionary is passing, and revolution itself is being eclipsed by change.

We propose that humanity is moving beyond the story of revolution into a new era. Now humanity has entered the era of *evolution*. It is a time in which our conscious creation of human evolution is shaping all life on earth. We define evolution now as a process for which everyone has coauthorship and coresponsibility with nature and the sacred intention within life. Genetic engineering, life in earth orbit, destruction of the Amazon rain forest, global Internet communication, global warming, growing human freedom, toxic pollution of air, land, and water, emerging fascination with soul and spirit—there are countless signs that all of humanity as one being is beginning the most challenging renaissance and transformation in the history of our species. We are now becoming conscious cocreators with nature and of nature. As a result we are entering the most threatening and promising time in our history.

CONSCIOUS EVOLUTION

We call this an *era* of evolution because the gradual, peaceful development and unfolding of higher, more complex order that we define as evolution has changed. The acceleration of evolution makes more visible to us the rapid development of our global culture and the changes in our lives and our bodies. It is as though a fast-forward view of life is helping us see the bigger picture of evolution.

In this century, in the lives of one generation, humanity has evolved from travel by horse and wagon to walking and driving on the moon, from the heavy motion of huge sailing ships and ocean liners to weightless life in earth orbit. Our range of vision, thought, and action has expanded microscopically and macroscopically into nature and the cosmos almost beyond belief. The time has come when we must consider an evermore careful and active role in guiding our own evolution.

We must now seize the opportunity and responsibility for evolution rather than letting devolution prevail. The story of devolution, the denigration of evolution that culminates in species extinction, is the opposite side of the coin of evolution. The choice between working for healthy evolution or giving way to devolution through inaction is a decision everyone will make and is one of critical importance. Our hope in the era of evolution is that with humanity's growing level of knowledge and understanding, we can both see and comprehend evolution as it unfolds and opt for human fulfillment within enduring planetary health.

ACCELERATION OF EVOLUTION

Evolution in human life and culture is accelerating so fast and is communicated electronically around the world so rapidly that it is visible to us. We can literally watch evolution happen, both the devolutionary threat and the evolutionary promise. By satellite image, we can watch the destruction by fire and clearing of the Amazon rain forest terminating untold species of life. On the evening television news, we can watch the story of the first cloning of a sheep and wonder when the story will tell of human cloning. On the Internet, we can watch and participate in a conference creating new knowledge for the future of human spirituality.

In countless ways, we have all become actors in the physical and social process of human evolution itself. Just as we can trace the history of our species' evolution from *Homo erectus* to *Homo sapiens*, we can also follow our evolution from migratory tribes to nations of the world. What is so different now is that evolution has accelerated to the speed at which we can see it happen in the days and weeks of one lifetime.

One of the amazing things about the great cathedrals, such as the ones in Amiens and Reims, France, is that they required generations to complete. People needed a multigenerational view to understand their contribution. Now evolutionary events can occur and even be redefined within one lifetime. Many of us have evolved, for example, from seeing computers as huge, distant machines run by experts to using them as essential tools for our daily lives.

Because we can see evolution occurring, we can now seek to more fully understand it and be part of it. As participants in evolution, we gain new responsibility for defining what we call evolution and our own roles in it. Our choice now is to make a conscious, deliberate decision about our role in evolution. That is why we say that the era of our conscious cocreation of human evolution is dawning. The moment is at hand to join nature's many-billion-year-old cosmic success story as whole-earth humans working with and for evolution itself. Through historical circumstance, we are all heirs to the awesome opportunity and critical responsibility to become authors, guides, and actors in the future of human evolution.

THE EVOLUTIONARY

In response to the dawning of the era of evolution, a new human role is being called from within us. We propose that we transform the adjective *evolutionary* into the noun *evolutionary* to name a person who, in moving beyond the revolutionaries of recent history, seeks to work with and for the natural order of evolution itself. An evolutionary is a conscious, creative, compassionate collaborator with the future of life itself.

Beginning the search for ways to find the comprehensive compassion and wisdom to take on the role of evolutionary is a purpose of this book. There is a precedent for this search in the decision-making process of Native Americans who consider the effect of their current decisions on children seven generations into the future. Recent initiatives in environmental and ecological sensitivity, social responsibility, and economic and community sustainability are efforts in which the search for healthy evolution is under way. Even so, taking on the role of evolutionary and the search for how to proceed may seem presumptuous and arrogant, especially because we may feel ill prepared to become conscious collaborators with the ancient and sacred process of creation itself.

As writers, however, we believe it is critical to begin the conversation about the business of healthy and fulfilling human evolution, because it is being fast-formed all around us with or without our participation. We believe it is important and timely to bring our findings about growth, learning, and evolution to open consideration so that other evolutionaries may think through our discoveries and conceptual tools and, we hope, adapt them, work with them, and build with them. It is our choice to make the conscious decision to support healthy evolution.

CHIEF EVOLUTIONARY OFFICER

Whereas evolutionary work by its nature is collaborative and integrated, a synthesis of influences and actors, we see at the outset that evolutionaries are persons who take leadership initiatives first within themselves and then with others. Therefore this book is written to you creative, courageous individuals who are seeking to work with and for evolution. Regardless of your leadership position or location, if you are beginning your learning and self-defining as an evolutionary, we call you a *chief evolutionary officer* because:

You are the *chief* of your own soul and its worldly service in an ever-growing council of chiefs caring for the evolution of life on earth.

You are an *officer* in your willingness to carry the responsibility of learning to lead us into enduring partnership with the natural order of successful and fulfilling evolution.

You are an *evolutionary* because you make *evolve* an active verb. You work to develop and bring forth a higher order of natural grace and well-being for all life. By seeking to evolve yourself, you help to evolve with others their visions, values, situations, and organizations whenever quality of life is in question and in a state of potential for the enhancement of healthy evolution.

One thing chief evolutionary officers have in common as they take their visionary stand in times of renaissance, revolution, and evolution is a fascination with nature and a passion for seeking from nature's well of secrets clues to its deep-structure order. We share with you aspects of this passionate search from other chief evolutionary officers we have known and studied, such as Leonardo da Vinci, Thomas Jefferson, Margaret Mead, Barbara Hubbard, Buckminster Fuller, and Teilhard de Chardin.

A central purpose of this book is to tell you the story of our journey in the search for deep structure and natural order and to teach you how to use what we have found. Our intention is to help ground and guide your intentions to evolve by presenting our discovery of a process-pattern that nature and evolution always use. We provide a way of thinking and a method based in a natural process-pattern that you can use to enhance healthy evolution. From our discoveries, we show you a way to begin thinking for yourself in the way that nature and evolution think for themselves.

Thinking as nature and evolution think brings you to a new threshold, a new potential. For instance, an old assertion was that the business of business is business. The more recent knowledge era assertion is that the business of business is learning. Now the integration of your thinking with the stages and dynamics of evolution's makes possible the new assertion that the business of business is evolution. Such a profound transformation of purpose in all the global domains of creativity, enterprise, and commerce is essential and inevitable if we are truly seeking and accepting the responsibility for conscious human evolution.

World culture is moving beyond the scientific industrial era and beyond the more recent transforming information, knowledge, and communication era. A central question defining the emerging era of evolution is how to go into business partnership with the success processes of evolution, nature, and the cosmos. In all the domains of the business of living and regenerating life itself, how does human creative endeavor become conscious evolution? What does it take to build an enduring friendship with evolution itself?

We assert in this book that the answers to the questions of successful friendship and partnership with the processes of evolution require a natural transformative maturation of human values and intentions. The maturation process is natural because the higher values are already known to us in the depths of our souls and have already been enacted by the great spiritual leaders of all time. The whole next stage of human evolution is the era of conscious evolution. It is the transformation of the scientific industrial era into a union of our present capabilities with the emergence of our already indwelling social and spiritual fulfillment, the flowering of a higher-order unity of human values and intentions.

The four dynamics of transformative growth and development are gathering, repeating, sharing, and transforming. In the natural unfolding of our higher-order form of planetary living, these dynamics and the sequential process we call the METAMATRIX® are a guide to formation of new deep human values to enhance our evolution. Conscious use of these dynamics of growth as values and their ordered sequence as a value system offers a beginning point for conscious evolution and a beginning in the formation of new spiritual intention. After the stages of gathering, repeating, and sharing, the transforming stage always reveals a new higher-order ideal intention, and often a new level of ideal spiritual development.

We are convinced after hearing hundreds of success stories from all sorts of domains of creative endeavor that idealism is the mother of practicality. We know that ideal forms in nature are the enduring vessels of evolution. The search is underway in this time of renaissance to find the ideals of nature's creative process so that we can value and use this guidance as we begin to consider and seek the conscious evolution of our own human species. The discovered creative dynamics of the process of all growth, development, and evolution offer a starting point in finding new values and ideal intentions. They also offer a way to seek comprehensive wisdom and compassion so that we all can take on the role of evolutionary and the leadership role of chief evolutionary officer.

In addition to the valuable dynamics of growth and evolution, two more value systems permeate this book. Combined they help form a focus for the creation of ideal intentions. It seems obvious to us that an emerging era of evolution calls for an age of ideal intentions, a time when the highest aspirations and value assertions that we can make are necessary starting points, foundations for building conscious evolution.

The artist Carl Andre once said, "Art is what we do; culture is what is done to us." Although the era of evolution is becoming our world culture, perhaps our art of creation begins with our ideal intentions as evolutionaries and chief evolutionary officers. We suggest that using the dynamics of transformation allows us to consider a new art form of social architecture wherein we can intend, design, build, and become a second new value-based initiative: a *conscious, creative, collaborative, compassionate community* (C4 community). The four Cs are a value guide for both chief evolutionary officer leadership and for the creation of any endeavor, enterprise, or community. The C4 community values will

emerge in fuller detail as we progress through the four stages of the book.

The third explicit value system follows the four sections of the book and helps to focus each section. There are four value statements, radical in their form, brevity, and assertiveness. We have discovered each from the process of whole-domain mapping with the METAMA-TRIX®. These statements, derived from working insights, are stimulating ideals. Taken together as a mode of operation for chief evolutionary officers and evolutionaries, these statement form a highly challenging value code and guidance system for the creation of ideals in the pursuit of conscious human evolution. We call these statements the four *ideal intentions*. They complement and enhance the four Cs and the four dynamic stages of transformative evolution. These four ideals are the highest aspirations that have emerged from our work in future mapping and social architecture. If we did not offer them as our highest ideals, we would betray the magnitude and importance of the challenge of conscious human and planetary evolution. These ideals are as follows:

- Evolution is the only business.
- Life is the only customer.
- Community is the only profit.
- Love is the only future.

One ideal guides each of the four parts of the book. Now let us get on with understanding the creative dynamics of evolution.

2

Nature's Patterns of Success

In times of renaissance, people have repeatedly looked to nature for inspiration and ideals. Leonardo da Vinci looked for recurring patterns in nature such as the wavy ripples in a brook and the wavy curls of a woman's hair and sought ways of incorporating those patterns into his inventions. As he thought of flight for humans, Leonardo looked to nature for ways of achieving flight. In his sketches and inventions Leonardo included the patterns and processes that served nature well.

Thomas Jefferson, when he wanted to design a more effective plow for his fields, looked to nature for natural patterns of curve and curl. In reproducing one such curve in his plow, Jefferson produced a plow blade with superior capabilities for turning the soil. His design is still used today.

We find ourselves on the verge of a time of necessary rebirth and revitalization. We can see in the decay of our cities and social institutions, exemplified by the tragic killings in and around schools, that our way of life is not serving us well. We also can see that we are destroying the natural world around us. We are experiencing one of the most extreme declines in species the world has ever known (Wilson 1992). We cannot help but worry about what all this portends for our own species. Though we are not yet sure what we must do, we do know that how we live our lives, relate as communities, and run our businesses in the future will be very different from those activities today if we are to ensure healthy life on this planet.

One way of designing our future is to look into nature's deep-structure patterns and natural order to see how healthy evolution has prospered in the past. With that understanding, we can find ways of adapting nature's success to our own. Nature provides both the examples of success and the deep inspiration and awe to feed our human creativity. From that well of creativity, together we can surely design a healthy future.

In signing up to be chief evolutionary officers (CEOs) and in writing this book, Gus and I are offering our services in the cocreation with others of a healthy future. As we look at the lives of other CEOs and our past and future evolution as a species, we apply nature's deep patterns to frame our understanding and learning. The particular patterns we use are general periodicity and transformative growth.

PATTERN AND PREDICTABILITY IN GENERAL PERIODICITY

Periodicity is well known to us in chemistry, in which there is a predictable pattern of increasing complexity and order. In the periodic table of elements, discovered by Mendeleyev, we find such order in the atomic structure of elements. As Mendeleyev searched for a deep-structure relation, he arrayed his cards of all the known elements in ordered rows. By walking 90 degrees around the array, Mendeleyev discovered that a pattern occurred both horizontally in the rows and vertically in the columns. Because the pattern in this original discovery was so consistent, Mendeleyev was able to predict the existence of as-yet-undiscovered elements and the necessary attributes of the missing elements on the basis of the position of empty spaces in the array. His predictions told scientists what to look for, and soon the missing elements were discovered.

General periodicity then is the all-encompassing term we give to the growing and unifying collection of the discovered, predictable patterns and processes in nature. This deep-structure general periodicity is an overarching pattern that crosses domains, disciplines, and fields of endeavor. A generally periodic pattern or process is one that is used and reused throughout nature.

In their wonderful book, *By Nature's Design*, Murphy and Neill (1993) identify six patterns that nature uses repeatedly to create our physical world. These patterns include spirals and helixes, fractals, and branching, among others. The striking simplicity and the repeated use of these patterns gives us insight into nature's use of structure and its ability to create magnificence from simple patterns.

Nature also has a number of processes that it uses and reuses. Gravitational pull among orbiting bodies in our universe is a good example. The pattern of earth orbiting the sun is repeated in the orbits of the other planets and again in the orbit of the various moons around those planets. On a larger scale, scientists have discovered a star with characteristics similar to our sun. They believe that the clouds around that star are forming into planets through the same process as the one that formed the planets, including earth, around our sun. What this phenomenon suggests is that there is an all-pervasive pattern of general periodicity throughout all dimensions of behavior in time and space in nature from the formative spin of atoms to galaxies and from a human breath to human evolution.

Finding patterns and processes in nature helps us interpret the past and present and set our vision of future potential. The periodic table of elements is a good example. Seeing the orderliness of the atomic structure of atoms within the elements is both mentally and

emotionally comforting. Seeing the building blocks for everything in our universe arrayed in such deliberate order gives us a sense of being in an orderly, knowable universe. That integral array, even with its original gaps for missing elements, is a pattern of and symbol for order. It is also a predictive pattern for the future. Once the order was understood, other scientists had a blueprint of the missing elements to speed their search. In that way, the gaps became the predictors of future discoveries.

Just as repeatable patterns help us to fill in the blanks, a known and repeatable process gives us the ability to interpret what has occurred and to predict what will occur. In that very familiar process of human growth, we all know what the stages will be and that we will encounter all of them in order. Similarly, the order and pattern of our seasons, part of the process of our solar system, let us predict with great confidence and reliability that spring will follow winter every year.

TRANSFORMATIVE GROWTH

Transformative growth is an example of general periodicity and a central concept in Gus's creation of the METAMATRIX®, as he explains in Chapter 3. The theory of transformative growth is that everything that grows, learns, and evolves passes through a known sequence of stages. Because each distinct stage has its own unique dynamics, it is possible to predict the driving forces behind change in each cycle of repeated stages. Together the stages form a deep-structure process and pattern that is so pervasive that it guides learning, creativity, and growth toward the next higher order of being. This process-pattern is, therefore, also a description of evolution itself.

We call the four sequenced stages of transformative growth gathering, repeating, sharing, and transforming. These four stages form a process-pattern that repeats as growth and evolution continue. The completion of each stage of transforming enables the start of a whole new cycle. This sequence occurs through nature at the microphysical, biophysical, and macrophysical levels. For example, when a caterpillar hatches in miniature, grows to full size, enters a chrysalis, and finally emerges as a butterfly, it has completed a full cycle of stages in the transformative growth process. The earth-bound caterpillar suddenly is capable of spreading it wings and flying from flower to flower. It has transformed itself into a higher-order, more complex state of being.

Evolution is nature's strategic growth and health plan. With an understanding of transformative growth, an evolutionary has insight into nature's process-patterns and can put that insight to work in shaping a successful and healthy future individually, for an enterprise, and for humanity. Moving from the theory of transformative growth to a practical application in our thinking and daily lives and in our non-profit and for-profit enterprises is a critical shift to make. Turning our ideal visions of potential into a map that guides us step by step to a healthy future is the work of a CEO.

NATURAL ORDER AS A THINKING TOOL

Since the 1970s, Gus has been drawn to the potential of using natural order as a design pattern and planning process for human creativity and fulfillment. The idea of using natural models has long appealed to humankind, as we can see in the examples of Leonardo da Vinci and Thomas Jefferson at the beginning of this chapter. Gus's contribution to the use of natural models is the creation of a map that allows us to visualize the natural process-pattern of transformative growth. He has named his map the METAMATRIX® because it is a bridge between natural order and human thought processes set in the form of a matrix.

We can draw a number of implications from the creation of a METAMATRIX®. Most important, of course, is the ability to connect natural process-patterns to human thought in a visual form. With that capability, we can make a number of extensions, including the following:

- Arrayed analysis of any subject and its story and stage of natural maturation.
- Prediction of future growth dynamics and scenarios.
- Creation of ideal intentions by CEOs to bring out their best gifts of service.

As you will learn with the unfolding of our chapters, these capabilities are at the heart of this book. Both Gus and I use the METAMATRIX® because it is the most logical way to frame our messages for you and to provide an underlying consistency. This consistency helps us coordinate the coauthoring process. We hope it will also help you synthesize our messages about the hopeful and healthful evolution of life on earth.

THE METAMATRIX® MAP AND NATURAL ORDER

The METAMATRIX® map is an integration of the pattern and process of transformative growth into a visual map, as shown in Figure 2–1. It depicts the growth process in an interactive form that is a visual expression of transformation. The map is generic and broadly applicable and, therefore, describes the natural evolution of anything that grows, for example, groups, companies, or beaver colonies.

Each of the four stages of transformative growth is represented in a vertical column of the METAMATRIX® to allow expression of the dynamic unique to that stage. As with the human-life stages of infancy, childhood, adolescence, and so on, there is a necessary and predictable sequence of stages and creative behavior for each stage. Each stage is unique but incorporates and builds on the previous stage. In sequence, the four stages create one growth cycle in the continuous developmental and evolutionary process. We define the four stages as follows:

- *Gathering* is the process of forming a sustainable physical being or idea. Growth is achieved through an increase in size and ability. The same being or idea becomes larger and stronger.

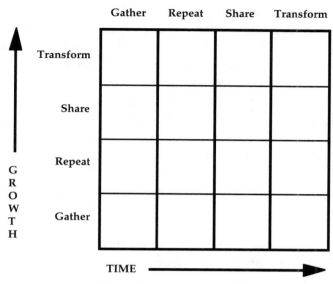

Figure 2-1   *METAMATRIX® Map*

- *Repeating* is the process of making multiple likenesses of a new being, product, or idea. Growth is achieved by the number of multiple likenesses repeated.
- *Sharing* is the process of expanding by integrating differences and increasing relationships. This process creates a richness, complexity, and synergy from the union of differences that is not seen in the repeating process. The result is greater than the sum of the parts.
- *Transforming* is the process of creating a higher-order union of increased potential. That is, what had been a caterpillar becomes a butterfly. This process totally changes the identity of the being, product, idea, or relationship.

Within each stage, we can take a more detailed view of development. We can also combine a series of maps to obtain a broader, ongoing view. We can use the map for both more expansive and more detailed thinking because a METAMATRIX® map is fractal in process and pattern. Each stage is internally consistent with the larger pattern of gathering, repeating, sharing, and transforming. Use and repetition of internal consistency is the definition of the word *fractal*. Each of the four stages contains the sequence of gathering, repeating, sharing, and transforming to form a smaller, fractal version of the larger stages. In fractal design, small parts are similar in structure to large parts and provide the same order within the larger order.

Nature commonly uses fractal design. Fern fronds are a good example, as shown in Figure 2–2. The basic shape of the fronds is similar to that of the leaves and, working down in size, of the leaflets. We can find similar relations in the veins of a leaf, the twigs, the branches, and the entire tree; all follow the fractal design. We can find the same fractal repetition in the ever-increasing size of the spiral chambers in a shell such as that of the nautilus.

We talk of the METAMATRIX® as a means of bringing natural order to our creative thought processes. This happens in two ways. First, the sequence of gathering, repeating, sharing, and transforming is in itself a natural sequence. Second, with the addition of the natural order of fractal progression, we extend the METAMATRIX® from a one-time process to a continuous process of evolution and creation. The fractal nature of the METAMATRIX® provides two-way creativity. In each smaller occurrence of the pattern, you can see increasing detail. In each larger occurrence of the pattern, you can see the next order of creative potential.

Figure 2–2   *Fractal Pattern of Fern Frond*

Generally speaking, the fractal form of the METAMATRIX® with its 16 sections provides a useful level of detail for analyzing and predicting growth. It is the form used most frequently throughout this book. Sometimes, however, a more basic four-column form is useful for overview thinking. At other times, connecting a series of maps for the big picture view is helpful.

FOUR-COLUMN OVERVIEW THINKING

Using the METAMATRIX® in four-column thinking is a basic application of its analytical and predictive capabilities. Given any situation or opportunity, we can see how it has or can evolve through the stages of gather, repeat, share, and transform. In our discussions, we use examples of four-column thinking to frame the stages of growth. We include Table 2–1 to give you a feeling for the growth and evolution that emerges as the sequence of gather, repeat, share, transform is applied with four-column thinking.

Reading down each column gives a good sense of the dynamics of gather, repeat, share, transform as they apply to individual growth stages across a variety of subjects. Reading across each row lets you feel the momentum of growth and change from stage to stage as life and learning unfold. Taken together, the four stages provide a complete growth cycle that ends in transformation and the opportunity to continue growing and learning at a new and higher point on the

Table 2–1 *Examples of Four-Column Thinking*

Field	Gather	Repeat	Share	Transform
Human development	Child	Young adult	Adult	Elder
Life of Jefferson	Youth	Practitioner	Leader	Sage
Human learning	Information	Knowledge	Wisdom	Enlightenment
CEO values	Conscious evolution	Creativity	Collaboration	Compassion

evolutionary map. In all instances, four-column thinking provides an overview of both past achievement and future ideal potential.

POTENTIAL FOR INFINITE GROWTH

Transformative growth is an ongoing process. We look at each growth cycle as having four stages. Growth, however, continues from one cycle to the next. Once the four stages of an individual METAMATRIX® are complete, growth has the option to continue by breaking out into a new cycle. This breaking out is always a move to the next higher order of creativity. That is, breaking out of one growth cycle and into the next is a fundamental part of the evolutionary process.

The application of the map for both analysis in increasing detail and for breaking out into newly defined contexts for continued growth is very useful to a CEO. Just as the METAMATRIX® is a bridge between natural process-patterns and human thought, the CEO is a link in the process-pattern of human evolution that leads to the creation of healthy life on earth.

APPLICATIONS OF THE METAMATRIX®

To help all of us envision and create a future with the greatest potential, we use the broadest possible context for our thinking. Throughout this book we put METAMATRIX® maps to work in examples that establish that context and provide the dominant themes of this book, which are as follows:

- The map of human evolution provides the broadest possible past, present, and future context for every discussion in this book. This is the context in which CEOs plan for our conscious evolution.
- Domain mapping is a METAMATRIX® process that helps CEOs envision and plan the successful growth of an enterprise in any domain of human endeavor, including businesses. Domain mapping shows how to create success in concert with healthy life on earth and takes place within the larger context

of the map of human evolution. Domain mapping is the heart of the second part of this book.

- The map of human learning shows the learning stages that we all may go through in our lives. Setting human learning in a METAMATRIX® map opens the possibility for comparing our development as a species and our development as individuals. The relations between both kinds of development provide CEOs with insights useful in planning conscious evolution.
- The map of social architecture shows the steps a CEO might take to design and create conscious, creative, collaborative, compassionate (C4) community. This map dovetails with the maps of human evolution and learning to provide an integrated view of our future human potential.

Each of these examples follows the natural-order progression of gather, repeat, share, and transform that is the evolutionary process-pattern of the METAMATRIX® map. More important, though, is the context that the map provides with these examples. The idea of a strong relation between human evolution, the growth of our enterprises, and how we learn as individuals sets an all-encompassing vision to challenge the thinking and spirit of all of us as we learn what it is to be a CEO.

3

Discovering a Pattern of General Periodicity

This chapter describes some of the relationships with mentors and colleagues that helped my search for ways to define and take on the roles of evolutionary and chief evolutionary officer (CEO). These people are models of wisdom and compassion who have influenced me to offer, with Sue, the ideas to begin the search for conscious evolution.

Here too is an account of the search for more clues to nature's deep-structure order. This search led to the discovery of a pattern-process of general periodicity in synergetic integrity with the principles of transformative growth and evolution. These discoveries and creations are the underlying story behind the synthesis of the METAMATRIX® mapping process so useful to evolutionary thinking and work.

The era of evolution challenges us and demands of us all a continuously evolving reverence for the potential of all life and the sanctity and grace of the gift of life. I believe that the process of natural human development and maturation leads us all in the direction of increasing compassion. The METAMATRIX® mapping process can help describe that natural maturation stage by stage.

To fulfill the challenge of our evolving the potential of all life, the era of evolution will ask each of us to look into the mirror of personal meaning and ask the ancient cosmic questions: Where did life come from? Why am I here? Where are we going? And what can I do to help?

My answer to the question of help begins its fulfillment in this book and, in part, takes the form of the METAMATRIX® map and its use for evolutionary thinking. In even larger part, my own role as an evolutionary and a CEO is inspired and shaped by the gifts of writing and of shared experience with other evolutionaries. They have, with their general values and specific insights, directly helped me seek and discover a pattern of general periodicity that begins to describe the process of evolution itself. It is a way that is deep and broad enough to be very useful in thinking about anything, including the future of human evolution.

In telling these personal stories of friendship and reading that led toward my discoveries and map making, I suggest qualities and values from my evolutionary mentors and colleagues that I consider key for any evolutionary in the making. I call my mentors and colleagues themselves CEOs because of their strength and individual initiative, vision, and compassion for others, the earth, and life itself.

The common thread that runs through these stories is that each of my mentors, in his or her own unique way, sees nature as a mentor to humanity. Each sees that in taking clues and initiatives from nature, we can all think with compassion and act with values that move us along the evolutionary path to greater fulfillment in our lives and relationships. A strong sense of the use of natural order as a thinking process guides the thoughts of everyone I mention in this chapter.

To begin, I have had the great good fortune to know and work with several leading futurist thinkers, among them Buckminster Fuller, Margaret Mead, and Barbara Hubbard. Each has made a unique and valuable call for evolutionary thinking and action for us all. I also have learned from the drawings of Leonardo da Vinci during my development as a painter, begun in earnest at the Rhode Island School of Design. There I began a fascination with the deep-structure patterns of nature and how they may be overlaid to create rich, multiple, interactive meanings. There my paintings were the forerunners of the synthesis created in developing the METAMATRIX® map and the art of whole-domain mapping.

My paintings were made of four layers depicting emerging stages of evolution. The first layer was pure sunlight overlaid with a second layer of organic plant-growth patterns. The third layer was industrial construction and structure patterns overlaid with a final stage of electronic circuit patterns. In the METAMATRIX® map, I shifted depiction of evolution to a generic open pattern of development with vertical and horizontal progressions of distinct stages, each with its own open space to allow reading of words in sequence. Both the painting and mapping share the intention of visually depicting the dynamics of our evolution.

The writings of Teilhard de Chardin have been an inspiration especially as they point to a spiritual convergence in the wisdom of the future of humanity and to the cosmic importance and power of love now and in our emerging civilization. Teilhard gives credence to our final ideal intention that "Love is the only future" and to the METAMATRIX® mapping of the transformation stage of our lives as spiritual human beings, both individually and as a species. One of Teilhard's most inspired prophecies says, "The day will come when, after harnessing space, the winds, the tides and gravitation, we shall harness for God the energies of Love. And on that day, for the second time in the history of the world, we shall have discovered fire." Amid all the tumultuous difficulties besieging our world, I believe the emerging era of evolution will see the dawning of Teilhard's prophecy.

I have received profound guidance from the words of Saint Francis of Assisi, Jesus, and Thomas Jefferson. Though they are very different men from different times in history, each sees natural order as a basis of creation. Their guidance will later inform our evolutionary thinking together.

I have visited Assisi and prayed there to Saint Francis, whose guidance speaks to the building of a new conscious renaissance and a new era of conscious evolution. Saint Francis, well known for his reverence for all life throughout nature, knows the value of love and its integral place in natural order.

I think of Jesus exhorting us to see the holy mystery and beauty in nature as our guide when he says, "Behold the lilies of the field, they toil not nor do they spin. Yet Solomon in all his glory was not arrayed as one of these." And he tells us that beyond the coin of the realm of Caesar, there is a coin of the realm of God which is love and which alone is its own reward. Lilies of the field are a better model for beauty and love than anything that riches can buy.

I have visited Thomas Jefferson's home, Monticello, with an interest in Jefferson's ability to lead us as a social architect and visionary. His guidance has been truly inspirational. Jefferson helped me define social architecture as the wisdom of the universe revealed in natural order used for the planning and enhancement of human fulfillment. Here is yet another call to heed the wisdom of nature's order in the creation of evolutionary work.

I have received encouragement and inspiration from the work begun by Rendle Leathem and hosted by Sid Parnes and Bill Shephard at the Creative Problem Solving Institute (CPSI) in Buffalo. CPSI convened deep-structure thinkers under the banner of general systems theory. Later, I introduce the CEOs who had direct input into the discovery and use of general periodicity and the creation of the METAMATRIX® map for evolutionary thinking at CPSI. At CPSI, we approached general systems theory as the search for the general principles of natural order and creativity.

Now I introduce three futurists with whom I have had the good fortune to work. They are important to me because of the strength of their call to our higher potential for all humanity.

BUCKMINSTER FULLER

In 1965, when I completed my master of fine arts degree at the Rhode Island School of Design and went to Phillips Academy to teach art, I had the opportunity to attend a conference for graphic designers in Carbondale, Illinois, called Vision '65. There I heard Marshall McLuhan speak on media and its meaning and Buckminster Fuller speak at length on his macroscopic view of how we were bound to make the world work as a single success story. Bucky blew the barn doors off my mind, and I have never closed them since. He was my first CEO.

When I was later hired to be the arts assistant to Reverend Seavey Joyce, S.J., the president of Boston College, I recommended that Bucky Fuller be a graduation speaker, which he was. He spoke of the power and importance of general principles and how a person can build a life of valuable service with the discovery and use of such principles. I remember the examples of leverage and synergy and ephemeralization, how we evolved by learning to do more with less, such as replacement of transoceanic cables with satellites. The idea of the search for general principles became a deep value in my soul. Now I put that search high on the list of assets for all CEOs to enable them to base their thought and action on natural order.

I went to visit Bucky in Carbondale, and we made arrangements with members of his staff to hold the second playing of his World

Game at Boston College in the summer of 1970. The World Game was Bucky's social invention. In it he used his Dymaxion map (Figure 3–1), which arrays the land from the tip of Africa over the north pole to the tip of South America as one large earth island. With Australia and other islands, the map makes the concept of the success of one world visible and workable. The game enabled teams of players to research the location of all the world's resources from metal ores to religions on one visible, connected surface and seek to make earth a daily success story of redistribution of the ample resources to meet humanity's needs of the day.

The World Game seminar at Boston College, opened by Bucky, started all the players on a six-week learning experience about "Spaceship Earth," as he called it, and the possibility of creating the Earth's own operating manual for all-win-for-all-life living. Instead of a global war room, our workshop and map room became a global earth-evolution room. The value of that level of magnanimous and

Figure 3–1 *Fuller's Dymaxion Map*

macroscopic thinking is what every CEO needs to begin to imagine, rethink, and make manifest. That level of thinking, beyond all the confining boundaries and hatreds, and the energetic enthusiasm and optimism Bucky brought to it is what made him such a preeminent evolutionary and CEO.

Bucky, like Leonardo da Vinci, was a tireless explorer of the depths of nature. He had a particular strength in the discovery of synergetic geometry, which enabled him to invent the geodesic dome and other more-with-less building and thinking strategies. At a congress I helped to host in Florence, Italy, I remember Bucky working in eight-hour shifts with a small bit of food and a short nap between shifts for almost three days and nights continuously to create the geometric tools and models he needed for teaching. He was then in his early eighties. None of the young helpers he drafted could keep up with him. In his work and teaching in Italy, Bucky made a new discovery that so amazed him that it literally knocked him over while he was teaching. His discovery was a new insight into the primacy of tetrahedral geometry in natural order.

Thinking with the timeless ideal that nature uses in crystals, snowflakes, flowers, seashells, and all forms is another CEO asset that Bucky revealed to us all. I have applied some of it to the META-MATRIX® map of growth and evolution (see Chapter 5).

Finally, lest Bucky be remembered and valued only as a great architect or engineer or geometrician, consider him a philosopher of love, another CEO essential. Bucky answered my CEO friend Seth Itzkan who asked him "Why is there love?" Bucky's answer:

> Love is there to serve mankind.
> Love is the guiding principle of cosmological evolution.
> Love is the bounding energy.
> Love is the guiding geometric principle.
> Love is mankind's manifestation of nature's omnidirectional integration.
> Love is nature's healing generator.
> Love is nature's steel. It is the link of infinite tensile strength.
>
> Man's creation of steel [occurred] through the synergetic union of individual iron ore components defined in three-

dimensional space by nature's cosmological divine principle ordering to create a new stronger substance, here-to-fore nonexistent on earth and with greater tensile strength than had previously been possible. And thus allowing the evolution of modern society through air travel, sky scrapers and the like, was for humanity, a beginning of another chapter of nature's love story of evolution—creating greater and greater links of physical and mental and spiritual connectivity to propel humanity consciously on the same magic carpet ride that the invention of tensile strength superior steel has done for the modern age. Love is the steel of the new millennium.

MARGARET MEAD

Margaret Mead was another colleague and mentor of mine, a wonderful CEO. We met at the first Future Week held at the Chattauqua Community in New York, where we were both on the team of visionary speakers. At meals, we talked about some of the key moments in the formation of new science. She had been at the founding meeting of the Society for General Systems Research (SGSR), and she had participated in a series of working conferences in which discovering and developing the principles of feedback and the science of cybernetics were advanced.

At the SGSR meeting, Margaret had suggested that the organization be run on the principles of systems theory and the system behavior they were discovering. The elegant integrity and simple profundity of that idea became an inspiration for me and for subsequent meetings we had at Margaret's apartment in New York City. We also began discussion of creating a system and perhaps visual technology that could take a health and vitality image and measurement of a whole group, village, or even society.

Work I had done in multiple-layered imaging in painting, film, and television experimentation and our discussion helped synthesize some of my later work on the map of general periodicity. Later I came to realize that using the map to analyze the health and future of organizations and domains of endeavor is one solution to the image technology Margaret and I were seeking.

By far the most important contribution Margaret made to me and the work of all CEOs into the future came in response to my asking her to attend the First World Congress of the New Age that I helped design and host in Florence. She had to decline for reasons of health, so I asked her to pose some questions we might consider at the congress. One question was how to stop runaway positive feedback, such as an arms race. But the question that has meant the most to me and, I think, is a continuous challenge to all evolutionaries, is Margaret's question and insight, "How do you create natural organic models in science instead of arbitrary manmade ones? The difference," she said, "is in the intention. Arbitrary manmade models have as their intention the manipulation and control of people. Natural, organic models have as their intention resonance and reverence."

Today, I can think of no better spiritual orientation to the sanctity of all life than posed in Mead's question and commentary. As evolutionary scientists and all other CEOs in all domains begin to work on genetic engineering, ecology, conservation, biology and biodiversity, organizational change, human development, and myriad other perspectives and domains of action that are combining to create our conscious human evolution, Margaret Mead has asked us to engage our human soul and spirit in this critical and compassionate work.

Mead has asked us to think with our hearts and souls as well as our brains and minds—to use our full intuition as well as our reason. Resonance is a whole-body feeling and intuitive knowing. Reverence is a feeling and knowing of the soul. Mead is asking us to base the whole future edifice of science and other emerging domains of life service on the full depth and ability of human thinking, knowing, discovering, and revering—body, mind, heart, soul, and spirit.

This is a wonderful and critical challenge to us all. In mapping and modeling the general periodic stages of transformative growth and evolution, I had begun with a simple depiction of the organic growth pattern in a graphic four-column map. It became a 16-square matrix. Then it became a matrix nested in a golden rectangle and spiral. Most recently it has become an even more organic series of spirals based on a pine cone and sunflower. Each step toward a more organic image has brought about an increase in joy and excitement among the model users. In this book, we follow this sequence from columns to the more organic golden rectangle and spiral (see Chapter 5).

Resonance with what we model and reverence for it—thank you, Margaret, for helping to set us on the path of conscious intention and compassionate creation in our evolution with nature and of nature.

BARBARA HUBBARD

Barbara Hubbard is another futurist thinker, evolutionary, and CEO who writes and speaks eloquently on the story of all evolution and our place in it. Three months into our final draft of this book, our friend Benny Reehl heard Barbara on the radio and referred us to her new book, *Conscious Evolution* (1998). What a huge lift we got from her beautiful, visionary call, so synergistic with our efforts. In addition to her book, Barbara's visionary and principled creative action has been a great inspiration to me, from her place at the National Democratic Convention as an independent candidate for the vice-presidency of the United States seeking to add a peace room to the White House to her ability as a social inventor.

I first met Barbara in Washington, D.C., when she and John Whiteside had invented and were hosting one of the first SYNCONs. SYNCON stands for synergistic convening. It was a meeting in the round that began with small, separate focus discussion groups on key topics of the future. The groups synthesized their work with that of other groups as the walls, like spokes of a wheel, were periodically removed until the whole number of small groups became one large group in sharing all their ideas and suggestions. It was a democratic, people-powered, future-planning process and usually was televised on local public television stations. One of the best I participated in was held in Portland, Oregon, and focused on the energy crisis of the early 1970s.

The most exciting event in which Barbara and I participated together was the future-oriented opening of the National Bicentennial Celebration. In 1975, I was president of the Boston-Cambridge chapter of the World Future Society and thought of the idea of synthesizing the SYNCON process with the traditional New England town meeting to create "Town Meeting 2000." I proposed the idea to the state bicentennial commission and to WGBH TV, the Boston PBS station, where I had been a video artist in the experimental studio. We all agreed to the town meeting idea, and Barbara combined her mobile video production bus and crew with my student crew from Boston College.

On Patriot's weekend in April 1975 while President Gerald Ford spoke from the bridge in Concord where the minutemen fired the "shot heard round the world," we began "Town Meeting 2000." From the dirt floor of the Harvard Track Cage, our combined crew telecast the two-day proceedings of the meeting to a New England audience who could participate and vote by telephone along with more than 200 delegates to draft the articles for the year 2000 from the circular meeting floor. The subjects of the articles ranged from art to political economy. A special newspaper covering the meeting and the vote on the articles later was mailed to interested people worldwide.

So Barbara and I and our numerous collaborative colleagues created a bicentennial celebratory call worldwide for broad public participation in the consideration and creation of the future. "Town Meeting 2000" was a piece of social invention and social architecture that highlighted the need for and the creation of a process-pattern for collaborative visionary thinking in beginning the work of conscious human evolution. We were all evolutionaries and CEOs at that focal point in time as were the minutemen revolutionaries 200 years earlier.

CREATIONS AT THE CREATIVE PROBLEM SOLVING INSTITUTE

All these friendly creative collaborations with Bucky, Margaret, and Barbara and the visionary values that we put forward together were present in the work with which I helped Rendle Leathem at the CPSI in Buffalo, New York. With the generous and tireless support of Sid Parnes and later Bill Shepard, we convened general systems theory "homebase" discussion groups to search for the general principles of natural systemic order and to explore the various patterns and models our members had discovered.

The model presenters were luminaries from a wide variety of fields. For instance, Stuart Dodd was a founding figure in sociology. Derald Langham was a plant geneticist and creator of geometric models called GENESA crystals for synthesizing different kinds of energy and ideas. George Land is an author and the first proponent of transformation theory and a renowned business and organization visionary. Itzhak "Ben" Bentov was a biomedical inventor and author and delightful lecturer on the physics of consciousness.

John C. Gowan was an educational psychologist and author and theorist on the highest states of human creativity and consciousness. His son, John A. Gowan is a researcher, theorist, modeler, and writer on organization in nature and on his breakthrough thinking on unified field theory.

Rendle Leathem is a master at synthesizing this deep-structure thinking from others and inventing his own depictions of his understanding and theory. That kind of synthesis and invention was what he and I had as our fundamental goal at CPSI and what I had the opportunity to develop as well. We knew that general principles by their nature had to be in synergetic agreement, "interaccommodative," as Bucky would say.

DISCOVERING A PATTERN

My own contribution of theory, model, creation, and mapping practice owes a great debt of gratitude to Rendle and the CPSI group, especially to John A. Gowan and George Land for their discoveries so often shared. There is special excitement and soul-felt joy in seeking to think deeply with nature and in making conceptual connections based on its ever integrating and unifying processes and patterns. The beauty of the elegant simplicity it sometimes reveals is itself a spiritual blessing to feel and behold. With profound gratitude for the divine grace revealed in natural order and for the broad and deep insight of my colleagues John Gowan and George Land, here is the story of finding a general periodic order and creating a mapping process for it and with it.

George Land made one of the greatest contributions to general systems thinking I have ever encountered. In his book, *Grow or Die: The Unifying Principle of Transformation* (1986), Land established transformation theory. He presented a process of growth, a process-pattern shared by "psychological and cultural processes" and "biological, physical, and chemical processes." He first described that bold and profound discovery of an underlying, unifying pattern for all growth in the three stages he termed accretive, replicative, and mutualistic. That is, growth by increase in size and sameness (accretive), by self-reproduced likenesses (replicative), and by a union of the combination and integration of differences (mutualistic).

In *Grow or Die*, George graphed a transition phase between the cycle of the three stages that repeat themselves again at a higher level of capability and organization. Later in *Breakpoint and Beyond* (1992), Land and Beth Jarman offer new terms for the growth cycles, such as *forming*, *norming*, and *fulfilling*.

Over the years of work that I have done with transformation theory and its own evolution, I have used the terms *gathering*, *repeating*, and *sharing* for the original terms *accretive*, *replicative*, and *mutualistic*. I have also given the transition phase between cycles its own stage and name, the *transformation stage*, to show four distinct stages of growth and evolution. At the end of the gather, repeat, and share stages, I have discovered that the resulting transformation of identity needs its own fourth stage to exemplify and offer a surprising, often totally unforeseen higher order unity of power and potential. That transformed identity then becomes the gathering unit for the next higher line of evolutionary growth. In our interest in the potential of human fulfillment, for instance, we are drawn forward by the fully transformed ones, by the great visionaries, the mystical, prophetic, and holy beings who transform our world and help define the transformation of what we can be and are evolving toward as human beings.

Therefore my use of transformation theory offers four stages of gathering, repeating, sharing, and transforming. This four-stage concept set the stage for work with John A. Gowan wherein we discovered a process-pattern of general periodicity throughout all of nature at all levels and scales of evolution. John, in working on unified field theory, found that a four-by-three matrix of order found in astrology helped him map a phenomenon of progressive development in nature from the smallest to the largest known elements in the universe—from the photon to the universe itself. (Unified field theory is a study in which scholars seek to unite the four physical forces of the cosmos: electromagnetism, the strong and weak atomic forces, and gravitation.) John A. Gowan laid out his discovery in a chart he called "Organization in Nature" (Table 3–1).

John's chart has four developmental lines each with the same four progressive stages in three levels of ever-larger organization—microphysical, biophysical, and astrophysical. Each line of development beginning with the photon starts with a formative unit that

Table 3–1 *Organization of Nature*

Creative Dynamic:	Gather	Repeat	Share	Transform
Level:	Unit	Pair	Group or Field	Compound or New Unit

Microphysical Realm (strong, electric, and weak forces; four quantum numbers in three dimensions)

Particles	Photon	Particle/ antiparticle	3 families of 4 particles; 3 forces in 4 dimensions	Baryon; confinement by gluons
Atomic	Baryon	Electron-photon pairs; lepton pairs; quark pairs	4 quantum numbers × electrons, protons, and neutrons	Atom; electron
Molecular	Atom	Electron shell bonding; inorganic molecules	Carbon: 3 alphas of 4 nucleons; 4 valance electrons in third shell	Organic molecule and crystal
DNA	Organic molecule	Double helix; base pairs	4 bases of 3 chemical groups	DNA

(right margin: G A T H E R)

Biophysical Realm (life force; four nucleotides coded in triplets)

Cell	DNA	Replication	Genetic code; 4 bases coded in triplets	Cell; membrane
Organism	Cell	Cell division	3 functions × 4 tissues	Organism; skin
Species	Organism	Sexual reproduction	Population structure × evolutionary fitness	Species; reproductive isolation
Gaia	Species	Speciation; hybrids and polyploids	Ecosystem homeostasis; 4 seasons of 3 months	Gaia; earth life Atmosphere

(right margin: R E P E A T)

Table continued on next page

Table 3-1 *Organization of Nature, continued*

Creative Dynamic:	Gather	Repeat	Share	Transform
Level:	Unit	Pair	Group or Field	Compound or New Unit
Astrophysical Realm (gravitation; four third-order equations)				
Star	Earth; Gaia	Earth-moon gravitational orbits	4×3 gravitational field	Star; fusion
Galaxy	Star	Binary stars; earth-sun	4 spiral arms $\times 3$ supernova generations	Galaxy; heavy elements
Star	earth; Gaia	earth-moon gravitational orbits	4×3 gravitational field	Star; fusion
Universe	Galaxy	Andromeda; Milky Way	4 dimensions $\times$ leptons, hadrons, and bosons	Universe; evolutionary time and space
First cause	Universe	Universe/ antiuniverse	Natural and divine law; 4 elements $\times 3$ qualities	First cause; energy, conservation, information

S
H
A
R
E

Copyright © 1989 John A. Gowan and August T. Jaccaci.

progresses to a pair phenomenon and next to a group or field phenomenon and last to an emergent compound or new unit that becomes the formative unit for the next line of evolution. This pattern of unit, pair, group, and emergent compound or new unit repeats throughout the three physical realms and levels.

When John presented his chart at CPSI and he and I discussed it, I knew by intuition that the extension I had made from George Land's three-stage theory of transformation into four full separate stages should and would be isomorphic—identical in structure and process in some way—with John's four stages. Using my terms *gather, repeat, share,* and *transform* as the four distinct creative dynamic stages of change, growth, and evolution, I proposed that those dynamics were the action and creative dynamics of John's four stages. My discovery and suggestion of isomorphic relation caused us to create a new double story of order and a new chart of organization in nature (Table 3–1). In the new chart, the unit is the gathering stage, the pair is the repeating stage, the group or field is the sharing stage, and the emergent compound or new unit is the transformation stage. The transformative emergent compound or new unit is always the building-block unit for the next line of four evolving ordered stages, and it has a rich, crystalline magic. I have noticed that its profundity and potential is often the seat of breakthrough discovery that may then be the source of Nobel Prize recognition. The discovery of the crystalline double-helix nature of DNA is a good example.

In my synthesis of the two aspects of developmental order, John and I began to see a pattern of periodicity—cyclical change, growth, and evolution—throughout all the size and time scales of nature. The suggestion of such a possible pattern of general periodicity underlying all behavior of evolving increasing order appeared to be revealing itself. We were beginning to fulfill Bucky Fuller's suggestion of discovering and using a new general principle. We were offering a pattern-process of general periodicity that had within it the creative dynamics of an expanded theory of transformative growth. As in the ideal definition of social architecture, guided by Jefferson, we were opening a new page of the wisdom of the universe revealed in natural order. Later in formulating the METAMATRIX®, I would take another step to use the newly found order for the planning and enhancement of human fulfillment. But first there was more to be discovered in the pattern of periodicity.

Recognition of the internal integrity of that emerging pattern of periodicity took another leap forward one day while I was listening to John present our new chart to a group at CPSI. I did what Mendeleyev did when he walked 90 degrees around his array of cards in rows depicting the qualities of the known elements. By doing so, Mendeleyev discovered order running vertically among the elements as well as horizontally. This discovery provided Mendeleyev with more information about each element, especially the missing elements, which were soon discovered.

As John was speaking about our table of organization in nature arrayed on a single piece of paper, I turned the paper 90 degrees. In so doing, I discovered that the whole universe of order, the whole table from photon to the entire universe, was ordered in both directions with self-similar stages within stages. The whole universe of order on our chart is a gather, repeat, share, transform phenomenon with the same sequence of staged order within order exhibiting the fractal nature of elegant simplicity in the design and process of all transformative growth and evolution. As labeled on the right edge of the chart, the microphysical realm is the gathering stage, the biophysical realm is the repeating stage, and the astrophysical realm the sharing stage. The transformative stage is the metaphysical, or nonmanifest, realm wherein lie the formative forces and processes that create the physical universe we know. This fourth stage does not appear on John's 1989 chart.

It occurred to me that I could and should create a simple content-free depiction of general periodic order to see what its creative dynamics could do to serve, enhance, and fulfill any subject as a guide and prediction of its growth and evolutionary behavior. That creation of what I have come to call the METAMATRIX® map and its use and its story of past, present, and future human evolution is the subject of Chapter 5.

4

Converging Paths

While Gus was working to develop his understanding of general periodicity and establish it in the general thinking and analysis tool he named the METAMATRIX®, I was building my skills as a technical writer, then manager, and finally leader of an information enterprise. This is the story of my career and how our two paths converged.

My story is also an application of the METAMATRIX® as a tool for looking back at my career to the growth pattern it followed and looking forward to my future growth and evolution. This application is a useful way of analyzing my career and will help you gain a feeling for the growth dynamics of the gather, repeat, share, and transform cycle.

GETTING STARTED

Starting in 1966, I worked for 29 years in the computer industry. Over that period of time, I joined three companies. First, Honeywell, Inc., hired me as a newly graduated English major and gave me my start. There I learned the trade of a software technical writer and the rules of traditional hierarchical management. It was a gathering of fundamentals.

TECHNICAL WRITING

At ENTREX, Inc., I experienced the excitement of an entrepreneurial start-up company. I was the twenty-seventh person to join the company and learned about the teamwork it takes to build a viable company. The can-do attitude of the whole company made it a special place to be in spite of the uncertainty of its being a start-up company in a shaky financial position.

In 1973, I joined Digital Equipment Corporation (DEC). There I worked and learned for most of my technical writing career and all of my management career. If I were to pick my most valuable experiences at DEC over that 22-year period, I would choose one from my writing career and two from my management career.

As a writer, I worked with the software team that designed the VAX/VMS operating system to create the design specification from which the operating system would be produced. The high quality of both the design and the resulting system, combined with the popularity of VMS among customers, left me feeling that I had participated in a very worthwhile process of design and act of creativity. Working as a writer at all three companies gave me both professional proficiency and recognition for my accomplishments. It was the repeating phase of my career.

THE PATH TO LEADERSHIP

I started my management career as a writing supervisor of eight people in 1979. In 1982, I made the transition from being a writing supervisor to a manager of 150 people writing, editing, and publishing a large portion of Digital's user-oriented technical documentation. I called the group Corporate User Publications (CUP). By the early 1990s, the group had grown to 1,400 people in the United States and Europe and included course development and instructional design as well as documentation. I renamed the group Information Design and Consulting (IDC).

As a manager at DEC, I had a lot of leeway in determining how I wanted to run my organization. As a result, I chose a business model that treated the organization like a small company within the parent company. With success, the organization became large and diverse with an annual budget of up to $96 million.

Having the freedom to run my organization as an independent company provided me with a wealth of learning experiences and opportunities. Because the group sold its services throughout the company to receive its funding, the size of the group was one measure of its professionalism and ability to meet internal clients' needs as well as external customers' needs.

Our ongoing growth reflected success. Other publications groups within the company asked to join the organization, and a few were acquired through corporate reorganizations. I managed the group carefully, always meeting financial targets in a rapidly changing environment. Financial responsibility was my ticket to independence and continued growth.

I think of my work as a manager and then leader as the share stage of my career. My style of management always included others in management decisions. My staff, their staffs, individual contributors, and our funding clients within DEC all had input into the management processes and decisions. In addition, the continuing growth of the group and the subsequent expansion of the management team provided an ongoing opportunity to bring new ideas and new blood into the organization.

That scenario of bringing in new ideas and people is the integration of differences typical of the share stage of growth in a METAMATRIX®. I think of this time as the sharing-repeat (S_r) stage of my career. The organization for the most part ran smoothly. I structured the management team, as was customary at that time in DEC, in a traditional hierarchical manner with four levels. Figure 4–1 places my career growth in a METAMATRIX®.

In 1990, with the inclusion of course developers and instructional designers from the training group into my organization, I was faced with the age-old challenge of merging two different functions with two different cultures. To me it was critical to recreate the organization to find synergistic strength, to build future skills, and to endorse a culture that supported both. People within the organization needed both new opportunities and a new culture to which they could move with hope and optimism if we were ever to make an integrated, functional organization from two formerly competing groups.

Added to the challenges I set for myself was the larger corporate environment. DEC had decided that it was necessary to reduce the number of people in the company. So while redesigning the organization and

	Apprentice Gather	Expert Repeat	Leader Share	CEO Transform
Transform	Wanting new opportunities	Decision to enter management	What next?	T_t
Share	Learning to be managed	Writing VMS design spec	Redesigning for individual creativity	T_s
Repeat	Learning to write technical manuals	Writing in a large and growing company	Managing a successful and growing business	T_r
Gather	Learning technology	Writing at a start-up company	Learning to supervise	Writing this book

GROWTH ↑

TIME →

Figure 4–1 *METAMATRIX® Map of Career to Date*

creating a new culture, my management team was also laying people off. In many ways, the layoffs contributed to the difficulty of the task. In other ways, the pain surrounding the layoffs heightened our awareness of the importance of making changes if the company were to survive.

With the support of organizational consultants and a design team from within the organization, I led the group through a transformation that resulted in a leadership model of management that was much less hierarchical than traditional organizational structures. It featured shared responsibility throughout the organization and greater empowerment of people doing clients' work.

In redesigning the organization, our underlying assumption was that our people were intelligent, responsible, creative, and knowledgeable. Working in teams (for example, writers, artists, and instructional designers) they brought a diversity of skills and an understanding of the client's work to a wide variety of projects. With access to the necessary information (for example, group goals and vision, budgets, and schedules), each team could produce a good information product and satisfy, even please, our clients without being told "how it needed to be" by management.

People empowered to think and make decisions need less managing. My goal was to move to a leadership model away from our traditional management structure. Through an open interview process, I hired a leadership team with whom I shared the responsibility of guiding the organization. The leadership team had collective responsibility for running IDC as a successful business and individual responsibility for developing excellence in functional skills. In this way, we balanced the growth of the organization with the growth of people's skills. Each leader was responsible for a number of coaches. Each coach was responsible for about 20 individual contributors.

With the move to coaches, the ratio of individual contributors to managers and supervisors changed from 10:1 to 20:1. This change resulted in a reduction in our costs that was appreciated by our clients. More importantly, coaching rather than supervising made people responsible for their own work and their careers.

For the most part, we were able to reposition excess managers and supervisors as individual contributors. Some, not wanting to make the change, left the organization. And, though it was never part of my plan, a few were moved out the door because of layoffs. That was, after all, the larger corporate goal and environment.

The recreation of CUP as IDC was a considerable effort that took more than a year. It changed the role of everyone within a large organization. Yet we never missed a beat. The group's level of professionalism was such that we met every deadline, produced high quality information products for our clients and DEC, and gained new work in the process.

This time of reinvention and creation is the sharing-share (S_s) stage of my career. In creating teams, empowering people, defining and enacting leadership, and loosening up on power and control, we created an environment that drew on differences in both professional skills and personalities to see the creative potential in our work. A shared vision of the culture that we wanted to create provided the glue that held the organization together and guided individual decisions.

WHAT NEXT? THE BEGINNINGS OF TRANSFORMATION

Once the new organization was in place and settled, I decided that it was time to start a new career. As part of a job-search process, I met Gus. My husband, Bill, saw an article in a local newspaper about Gus's campaign for governor of Vermont. I decided to write to him.

As I learned Gus's ideas about the use of natural order and predictable cycles, I became fascinated with both the theory and its applicability. The concept of predictable cycles and the conclusion that one could foresee and even design the future particularly caught my interest and imagination. I started asking Gus about the practical business applications of the METAMATRIX® and found his answers very engaging. Bringing the concepts of predictable growth to business development is my motivation for writing this book and the start of the transformative stage of my career.

As it turned out, Gus has a house of his own design, modeled on natural DNA patterns, in Thetford Center, Vermont. By coincidence, that was the very town to which the Bill and I were in the process of moving. Thus began a good and enduring friendship and the start of Gus's and my partnership as Social Architect Associates.

A question you might ask at this point is how I decided to start on the path to becoming a chief evolutionary officer (CEO). The answer lies in losing my way and then building a new path into the future. As part of my job search, I sent out resumes to a number of companies that interested me, heard back from some, and started interviewing. I found that I did not bring much enthusiasm to the interview process and that the jobs under discussion held little interest for me. Pity my poor interviewers!

As I started to analyze the situation, I realized that I simply did not want to be managed anymore. I didn't want a boss. After 29 years of being managed by people with a wide variety of capabilities at the job, I had simply had enough. This little epiphany of mine was quite a shock and very career limiting. After all, in corporate America everyone works for someone. It would take some courage and planning and lots of questioning and letting go (both characteristics of the transform stage and substages of the METAMATRIX®) to create a vision of how life as a self-employed individual might look.

In the end though, Bill retired and I left Digital and we started a new life in the hills of Vermont. I walked away from the prestige and secure income of a senior management position. We sold our house in Massachusetts and moved into our much smaller second home in Vermont. We also sold and gave away many of our possessions and left the neighborhood where we had lived for 25 years. We have never had any regrets.

Bill and I now work at our antiques business, which has been a shared passion for as long as we can remember. Gus and I work as founding partners of Social Architect Associates to spread the word about the benefits of having nature as a business partner. Combined, the two areas of endeavor give me a rich and challenging life.

Our home in Vermont is part way up a hill and overlooks the Ompomponoosuc River Valley. The Ompomponoosuc is a tributary of the Connecticut River that forms the border between Vermont and New Hampshire. It is a rural area and one where wildlife abounds. I have always preferred to be in the country. Now sitting amid nature provides an ideal setting for thinking about the kind of future I want and how to use natural order as a model for a new life. It is the ideal place, set in nature, to think about what it means to be a CEO.

CHIEF EVOLUTIONARY OFFICERS IN BUSINESS

Gus has given us a broad and inspirational view of who a CEO is. With my background, I find application of that view to the leadership of an enterprise practical and interesting. That is, I'd like to focus Gus's definition of a CEO on enterprise leadership at all levels in both the business and nonprofit sectors. In particular, I'd like to examine the high-level values held by a CEO and how these values play out in visionary leadership.

VALUES OF A CHIEF EVOLUTIONARY OFFICER

One way of describing a CEO is as a conscious, creative, collaborative, compassionate evolutionary working with nature and humanity for the success of all. Restated, we would describe a CEO as valuing

- Conscious evolution
- Creativity based in natural, organic pattern-processes
- Collaboration with life
- Compassion for life

Taken together, these four Cs form a value set that expresses our ideal for a CEO. They also express our ideal for the larger society, which we call C4 community and in which the CEO is an active cocreator and participant. Taken together, the values of a CEO and C4 community provide a setting in which CEOs can integrate the success of their enterprises with the success of healthy communities. As discussed in the third part of this book, the success of a business and its community go hand in hand with a set of values based on the four Cs.

CONSCIOUS EVOLUTION

A CEO is above all a conscious evolutionary. Gus describes a CEO as taking a visionary stand in times of renaissance, revolution, and evolution. The two phrases *conscious evolution* and *visionary stand* go hand in hand and complement each other. Both establish use of the broadest view and the biggest picture in setting a course for the future. That broad, evolutionary view implies taking responsibility for healthy life on this planet as we set the strategies for building the future of our communities and our enterprises. Native American wisdom is that in all our decisions we should consider the impact on the next seven generations so that we do not compromise future viability for temporary gains.

Taking a stand as a conscious evolutionary is a commitment to the ongoing process of healthy life. An important part of being a CEO is the development of a vision for the future of healthy life. This visionary aspect of CEOs, driven by the high ideals of the four Cs, becomes the force that makes CEOs inspired and inspiring leaders.

Using nature's process-patterns in creating and refining their visions gives both a rational framework and a method for a strong visionary future.

In the second part of this book, we look at the domain-mapping application of the METAMATRIX®. The purpose of domain mapping is to analyze current trends within a domain and to predict the future of the domain guided by the overarching ideal of providing a service to humanity. Domain mapping is the CEO's tool for envisioning the healthy and profitable evolution of all sorts of human endeavor, including nonprofit and business enterprises. In all cases, the value of conscious evolution is the cornerstone of a CEO's thinking, visioning, and planning.

CREATIVITY

All successful enterprises depend totally on the creativity of their members throughout the organization. Particularly in the age of the knowledge worker, the ability to synthesize diverse information into a new framework is an essential source of new ideas. These ideas lead to new products and services and other innovations that are the basis of the success of the enterprise.

CEOs know that in developing their own creativity and in fostering it in others they can have no better business partner than nature. As Gus has said, having a fascination with nature and a passion for seeking clues to its deep structural order is a quality of a CEO. When we look at the work of Thomas Jefferson, Buckminster Fuller, Margaret Mead, or any number of other CEOs, we can see the role that natural, organic patterns and processes played in their thinking and how these patterns and processes contributed to their creative genius.

COLLABORATION

Collaboration is the phenomenon that makes the whole greater than the sum of the parts. Of all the values held by CEOs, collaboration or teamwork is the one currently receiving the greatest play in the business world. Enterprises around the world are instituting teams of people as the best way to approach work. Each collaborative unit brings together a diverse set of individuals and values the contribution of each member. The integration of differences gives teams their leverage.

Collaboration, under the name of symbiosis, is a natural phenomenon. For example, birds on the backs of migrating cattle obtain food by eating pests on the cattle and receive a measure of protection through association with the larger beast. In return, the cattle are rid of bothersome insects. The synergy resulting from collaboration in nature, within enterprises, and among enterprises goes far to improve the quality of life and profitability of all concerned.

COMPASSION

In moments of compassion, we think with our hearts and souls. When we have compassionate thoughts and feelings, they often seem suprarational in that we use our caring, sympathy, and empathy for and with others to supplement our rational processes. Compassion extends beyond simply feeling sorry for one another to being willing to help. When we help others and when we receive help in times of need, compassion satisfies our mutual need for community. Compassion is a fundamental expression of the interrelatedness of life.

For CEOs who see the broadest evolutionary picture, compassion is a form of love based in the interrelatedness of life on earth. A rich and healthy life for humanity on earth depends on the great diversity of the other species of animals and vegetation with which we share this planet. We know that those species depend on what humans do. The power to evolve or devolve is in our hands. The result indicates that showing compassion for other species is, in effect, caring for ourselves. Compassion and caring for all life then become both a practical matter and an enactment of love for life.

VISIONARY IDEALISM

Thomas Jefferson is, after more than 200 years, a hero in the United States and in many other countries around the world. He was able to integrate his ideals for personal freedom with a vision for a new country that held those ideals as fundamental rights of the people. This visionary idealism made Jefferson an important figure during his life both before and after the American Revolution. The timelessness of his vision, based on principles he held most dear, makes Jefferson a symbol of freedom just as important now as he was centuries ago.

Though we are all troubled by his vacillation on the subject of slavery and his failure to free his own slaves, we can still find inspiration and purpose in Jefferson's expressions of human rights. Those expressions, such as the Declaration of Independence, have moved this large and complex nation to an ever-expanding understanding of personal freedom. We see the value of that freedom to all individuals, both at home and abroad.

Jefferson through his visionary leadership helped to move humanity along the evolutionary path. He did not do it alone, but he certainly made a substantial contribution to founding this country on ideals of human freedom. The important point for us is that visionary leadership at all times and in all types of enterprises has an impact on human evolution. As CEOs, we are all choosing to have an impact.

Businesses are among the enterprises that have had a profound evolutionary impact on society. We often debate the effectiveness of our local, state, and federal governments as agents of change. We also question the ability, and in some cases the appropriateness, of other social institutions, such as schools and churches, to be forces for change. Businesses are, however, uniquely situated to cause and profit from social change. They have the entrepreneurial freedom and the financial resources to have an enormous impact. Chief executive officers are uniquely positioned to be chief evolutionary officers. If we look at business, we can find numerous examples of business leaders who have changed our world. These leaders are always people with passionately held visions for the future they want to create.

DEFINITION OF VISION

Business literature is filled with the importance of having an overall vision to guide entire enterprises or groups within them. Peter Senge's *The Fifth Discipline* (1994) and Max Depree's *Leadership Is an Art* (1989) are excellent examples. Yet for all the emphasis on vision, the actual visions published for many enterprises are more of a wish than a guiding principle. We often hear "our vision is to increase sales by 20% over the next two years." Though such a statement is a worthy goal, it is not visionary.

A vision is a statement of ideal intention that inspires and motivates the vision's creators and all who are exposed to it. The vision is a picture of how the future might look. That future is painted in a way that helps everyone see the ideal good in making the vision a reality. In a very real sense, a vision is a statement that helps all involved see how to be their individual best as they collectively strive to make the vision a reality. Most often a vision is a statement of evolution and social change that does not seem possible when first presented.

EXAMPLES OF PAST VISIONARY LEADERS

When Steve Jobs and Steve Wozniak first set out to found Apple Computer, their vision was the creation of a computer that was accessible to everyone because of its ease of use and affordability. When they first expressed their vision in the 1970s, most of us had no clue as to why we would ever want to buy our own computer. That vision, however, had the power to change and enrich people's lives. It had the strength to grow a company and then an entire industry as other hardware and software manufacturers jumped on the bandwagon. Now the personal computer is a reality in households around the world.

Generally speaking, visions for evolutionary change have little impact unless the visionary leader has a passion for making them realities. Most of us have ideas for how we might make the world a better place but without committed action these ideas have little impact. Willingness to take a visionary stand is critical. Without Henry Ford's passion for making his vision a reality, his ideal of manufacturing a car that every American could afford would never have come true. Yet with his fierce determination, Ford not only achieved his vision and started Ford Motor Company but also opened vast opportunities for the entire automotive industry.

CHARACTERIZATION OF THE CHIEF EVOLUTIONARY OFFICER

Leaders such as Jobs, Wozniak, Ford, and others had a real impact on the evolution of modern life. There is no doubt that personal computers and affordable personal transportation have caused profound change in how we live and work today. Yet their evolutionary impact falls short of a CEO's impact in a very important way. For Jobs, Wozniak, and Ford, evolution was a by-product of their passion and vision. Evolution was implicit in their visions but not a direct, conscious goal.

For a CEO, creating conscious evolution is the goal, and the products or services offered by an enterprise are the means to that goal. Our human inclination to think in terms of conscious evolution is relatively new and fed to a large extent by the acceleration of the rate of change in society. Because we can now see evolution happening, we can begin to assume responsibility for its continuation as a positive force for all life.

With this important distinction in mind, we can start to characterize CEOs as having the following:

- A set of high ideals, such as consciousness, creativity, collaboration, and compassion, to guide their vision and actions.
- A consciously evolutionary vision or ideal future that they want to create.
- The passion and commitment to launch a renaissance and see their vision through to cultural acceptance and reality.

Taken together, these three characteristics form the why, what, and how of conscious evolution and are fundamental to the wise leadership of a CEO. By combining these characteristics with the staged development of natural growth and creativity, a CEO enjoins nature as a business partner in the creation of conscious evolution.

5

Creating the METAMATRIX®

The creation of conscious evolution is the most profound challenge humanity has ever faced. How to think as a friend and colleague of and with nature is one place to begin the challenge of awakening a search for conscious evolution. The discovery of a general pattern of periodicity and its stages of transformative growth offers us just such a preliminary thinking process. It is a process that works in harmony and resonance with the general dynamic of evolution itself.

Putting this thinking process in your hands as an aspiring chief evolutionary officer (CEO) is our purpose in presenting my story of the creation of the METAMATRIX® map. The map abstracts the dynamics of growth and evolution for general use and application to any subject. Its use is exciting as a way to begin considering conscious evolution. The METAMATRIX® map is a tool for predicting, designing, building, and becoming the natural unfolding of the highest and healthiest forms of evolutionary creativity possible.

CREATION OF THE METAMATRIX®

The descriptive and predictive power of a process-pattern of general periodicity and its creative dynamics of transformative growth stages are arriving in our history just when we need them most. We need an overview and creative orientation to our evolutionary future and the gifts already within us to bring about our successful partnership with nature and its long story of evolution. The METAMATRIX® mapping process is a beginning in that work of long-range vision and human inquiry into our roles as conscious evolutionaries and CEO leaders.

The search for universal process-patterns to help inform our thinking about the future of human evolution was and continues to be a search for synthesis of theories and chartings. As I have mentioned, I am a painter and my form of synthesis is primarily visual. Over years of work at the Creative Problem Solving Institute, I compiled a chart of

the many models with which we worked just to be able to see them all at one glance on one surface and to see the comprehensive picture.

A natural outgrowth of the work at the Creative Problem Solving Institute was my own work on visualization of our overview of general periodicity in which I integrated and refined the work of Gowan and Land. After I synthesized my four-stage chart of transformation dynamics with Gowan's chart of order in nature, I became convinced that the emerging pattern of self-similar stages within stages was a way nature thinks, forms, and processes growth. The four-stage process-pattern of transformative growth was for me a way to think as nature thinks.

I then decided to create a thinking tool to help others and myself apply that process-pattern of thinking. I started by creating a map devoid of all specific content except the unique creative growth dynamics of each of the four stages and their internal stages, sixteen in all, as shown in Figure 5–1.

Because I worked for years as a painter synthesizing organic plants, industrial machines, and electronic circuit patterns into simple

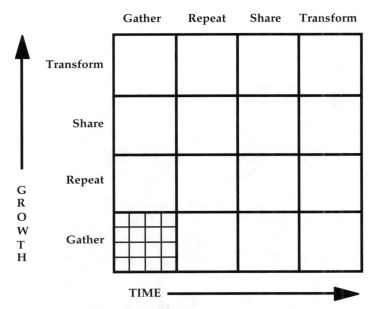

Figure 5–1 *METAMATRIX® Map in Sixteen Stages*

multilayered geometric shapes, I drew on those experiences. I decided to arrange the emerging pattern of general periodicity in a simple four-by-four square made up of the sixteen small squares. The result combines in one visual map the fractal growth pattern so prevalent in nature and the rigorous process of human thought.

The map reads from the lower left up each column. Each small square has its unique creative dynamic coded within it, starting with G_g, for gathering-gather. It soon became obvious that each small square could also be depicted with all sixteen squares within it, as shown in the gathering-gather stage of Figure 5–1. Although that depiction would yield too much complexity at the outset, it does point to the beautiful elegance of nature's fractal process-pattern within process-pattern.

The potential use of the order within order in each small square is similar to the way even a small piece of a hologram can project and form the larger whole image of which it is a part. I decided to call the sixteen-square map the METAMATRIX® because it depicts one over-arching metaview, a matrix of creative dynamic order within order applicable to any subject and story of growth and evolution. This application is true, according to the organization of nature chart (see Chapter 3) from which it is derived, down to the consideration of human life and on to the smallest things and actions we can discover.

To enhance the map further and show its own evolution as it is used, I placed the square map in a more organic context for its own potential motion of growth. I placed it in a golden rectangle. The golden rectangle and the spiral it generates are figures and patterns of archetypal growth in nature and in evolution. Therefore they make a good map pattern and process for any story of growth and evolution.

A golden rectangle has the golden mean proportion—1.618 for the long sides and 1.0 for the short sides (Figure 5–2). If you remove the 1-by-1 square from the rectangle, the remaining piece is itself a golden rectangle in the same proportions as the larger one, as shown in Figure 5–3. You can continue taking a square from each subsequent golden rectangle. The proportions of all these rectangles are identical. The diagonal line demonstrates the proportionality between two golden rectangles.

You can also add a new square based on the long side of a golden rectangle, and the whole new shape becomes a larger golden rectangle. The edge of each progressive square used as a radius for a quarter-circle arc generates the curving archetypal growth spiral found in sunflowers, pine cones, seashells, the formation of a hurricane or spiral galaxy, and numerous other forms in nature. This spiraling geometric pattern is itself an archetypal fractal progression called the *Fibonacci spiral* (Figure 5–4).

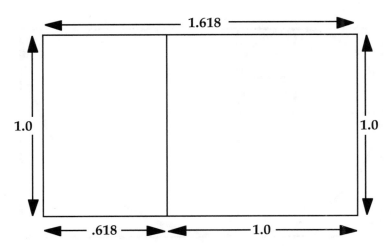

Figure 5–2 *Proportions of the Golden Rectangle*

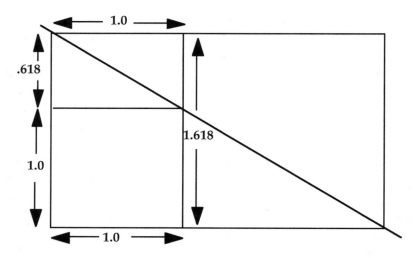

Figure 5–3 *Rectangle Divided into Square and New Golden Rectangle*

With a sixteen-cell square nested in a golden rectangle and tra-
versed by the archetypal growth spiral, I had created the METAMA-
TRIX® map, a thinking tool for considering the past, present, and
future of any subject as it increases in order and evolves. Because each
of the sixteen squares has a totally different dynamic made of creative
action, the differences help locate, describe, and predict the progressive

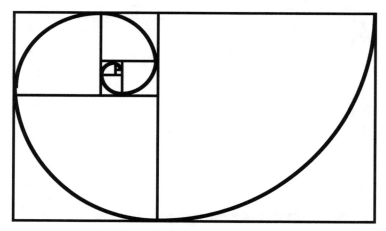

Figure 5–4 *Golden Rectangle with Spiral*

stages of growth and evolution. Figure 5–5 shows the METAMATRIX®
in a golden rectangle depicting a process-pattern of ongoing growth,
learning, and evolution.

As Gregory Bateson said, "Information is a difference which
makes a difference." That is what makes the sixteen-stage sequence of
different creative dynamics, from gathering-gather (G_g) to transforming-
transform (T_t), a powerful thinking and framing system for analyzing

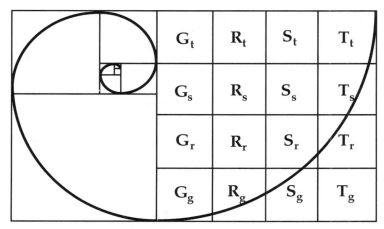

Figure 5–5 *METAMATRIX® in Golden Rectangle*

the present stage of maturation and evolution of any growth process for any subject. Even more important, once anything is located in the sequence of growth stages, all its near-term and long-term future stages of dynamic, creative action and behavior are arrayed in front of it on the METAMATRIX® map.

THE MAP OF HUMAN EVOLUTION

The METAMATRIX® map array means that for the first time general predictions and descriptions of the future are possible and reliable because the general periodic stages of growth are as dependable and predictable as the stages of human life or the seasons of the year. And, of course, the subject of human life, both as we live it individually and as our species unfolds and reveals its own story of evolution, is our focus of attention as the era of evolution dawns upon us and within us.

By far the most exciting application of the map is using it to study the story of human evolution, as shown in Figure 5–6. This map of human evolution contains the full story—our history from the dawn of our species to our current place in the information age to a vision of our full evolutionary potential. Using the synergy of the four-stage dynamics of gathering, repeating, sharing, and transforming, we have connected the past and present to our vision of the future. We offer it as our view for others to change, enhance, and build on as they choose.

For the time being we are devoting our attention to human evolution to date and its current place in the information age. Later in this book, we look at the full future potential of human evolution using our ideal intentions of community as the only profit and love as the only future as guiding values for our journey.

From our earliest origins as hunters and gatherers to our current global citizenry within the world of instantaneous electronic communication, the fundamental creative dynamics of how we live in the world are enactments of the sequential stages of periodic growth and evolution. We can see these dynamics playing out in the four columns of the map of human evolution.

What is not so apparent visually is the rate of our acceleration from stage to stage. Though the time lines vary from continent to continent around the world, it is generally true that the rate of change from

		Independent Nations	Collaborative Alliances	All-life Relations	Universal Love
Transform		Dark ages	Create conscious renaissance	S_t	T_t
Share		City-states	Information age	S_s	T_s
Repeat		Agriculture	Industrial age	S_r	T_r
Gather		Hunter-gatherer	Renaissance: science and reason	S_g	T_g

G R O W T H ↑

TIME ⟶

Figure 5–6 *Map of Past and Present Human Evolution*

stage to stage is increasing at an exponential rate. The ever-quickening pace as we awaken to our role as conscious evolutionaries is a source of astonishment and shock. It is important to keep this acceleration in mind as we discuss the map of human evolution.

The story of evolution took different routes on different continents. As different cultures developed in different places, cultural views and other local factors colored peoples' thinking and their subsequent evolution. What is important is that all civilizations evolved through similar stages though the time line varies. Now simultaneously almost everywhere we have all reconverged and are uniting globally in the information age.

It is also important to remember that each stage is carried along into the next and transformed by it. For instance, the agricultural stage has moved beyond animal-drawn plows to large tractors with computers and lasers aboard and satellite weather information to guide them. Our technology has changed how we plow, yet we go on growing and eating what we plant.

GATHERING STAGE OF THE SPECIES

In terms of the METAMATRIX® map, we began as hunters and gatherers at the gathering-gather (G_g) stage. There are still humans in remote areas of the world who live partially in that mode. And it is estimated that humans have lived as hunters and gatherers for a million and a half years or more, beginning in Africa and spreading out across the world to all continents.

Perhaps only ten thousand years ago, there was an evolutionary leap in the creative dynamic of human life to the gathering-repeat (G_r) mode with the invention of agriculture and the domestication of animals. The nature of human culture and settlement evolved as the nomadic patterns of hunting were replaced and village life began.

As settlements grew to large centers of exchange, the gathering-share (G_s) stage of human evolution emerged in the early cities of Mesopotamia nearly 5,000 years ago. The storage and sharing of food and the creation of numerous artifacts and skills brought about the sharing dynamic of the synergetic integration of differences and allowed our evolution into city-states and empires, such as the Roman Empire.

After the decline of the Roman Empire in the western world, we entered into gathering-transform (G_t), a time of transformation, the Middle Ages, 800 years of passage toward a new emergence of discovery and creative potential. Out of that era of crisis and retrenchment of knowledge came a transformation, a rebirth—the Renaissance and the flowering of visionary creativity and science.

Our evolutionary focus here is on developments in Europe. This focus derives from the fact that Europe, as it emerged from the Dark Ages (G_t), looked to the evolving sciences as the path for creating the future. As Europe and the western world created and drove toward the industrial revolution, nature became an object to be studied and controlled.

In eastern countries, on the other hand, nature was revered and, in some religions, equated with God. Not surprisingly, the western world led the way in creating the institution of science. That institution of science, so revered by the western world, eventually became a dominant influence on humanity and our evolution. Today the balancing influence of eastern cultural spirituality is increasingly entering western culture and helping to create a higher-order synthesis of meaning and being.

REPEATING STAGE OF THE SPECIES

The Renaissance and the birth of science started a whole new macrostage in human evolution beginning with repeating-gather (R_g). Science began a gathering of the repeatable principles and processes of nature, and we began a search for and partnership with that deep structure of nature's repetitions. The evolution of science moved rapidly for 400 years. With the grand synthesis of Sir Isaac Newton's cosmology, physics, and mechanics, we entered a new stage.

The era of the machine, repeating-repeat (R_r), emerged with manufacturing, industrialization, and mass production starting about 200 years ago. The creation of multiplicity became the main creative dynamic in the advanced nations of the world. Since then, we have been mechanically industrializing everything from food to knowledge, and R_r is now a worldwide creative dynamic.

Under the pressure of World War II just over 50 years ago, we entered a new stage and era of global repeating-share (R_s)—the repeated sharing of information. With the emergence of electronic communication with radio, television, and computing recently woven together with satellites, readily available information started to make a difference in people's lives. These technologies and numerous others working at the speed of light and electricity integrated the human brain and nervous system into a worldwide sharing of human thought and produced synergy, a world brain exemplified by the Internet.

The evolution of our technology is a story of the amplification of our human capabilities. Expanding technological capability first increased our muscle power to do work. It then increased the capability to create energy, to travel, and to help us see and hear more deeply. Finally technology gave us the present amplification of our ability to think and communicate worldwide instantly and to begin to explore in space. We have seen tremendous acceleration in the evolution of the stages of our dynamic modes of creation.

All our former stages are still with us at various places on earth. From our beginning as hunter-gatherers over a million years ago, the transformations of our evolutionary dynamic stages from G_g to R_s have occurred with increasing rapidity. Although these numbers are rough estimates, the acceleration is astounding: 1,500,000 years in G_g; 10,000 years in G_r; 5,000 years in G_s; 800 years in G_t; 400 years in R_g; 200 years in R_r; and 50 years in R_s. That acceleration in time and in technological extensions of our physical and mental capabilities has led us to another transformation threshold. Our current R_s stage of communication and information is only decades old and it is in transformation now. All humanity can feel the need and the pull from within for life-saving change.

We are entering the transformation stage (R_t) of the entire repeat column: the scientific-industrial, communication era on the map of human evolution. The time unfolding ahead of us is a conscious renaissance to create and usher in the era of conscious evolution. The possibility is at hand for a new grand synthesis that unites everything from technology to politics to economics to spirituality and all else into a higher order of being human. This light-speed world of human thought and action we live in, as it reaches its environmental limits of global industrialization and our growing population, is calling for a new human awakening, a new higher-order human as we begin to cocreate with nature the business of evolution.

The sixteen squares of the METAMATRIX® map of human evolution are mostly out ahead of us. We are now in the seventh stage, R_s. R_t and eight other stages are the future. Because they apparently are guided by superluminal human mental and spiritual principles and forces of creative dynamics, these stages operate beyond the speed of light and electricity in nonlinear time. This means that the acceleration of our evolution is potentially even more rapid than we have known because it is guided by thought and soul and spirit. Given this potential and the need for life-enhancing change, it is increasingly apparent that the real business of all our business is conscious, creative evolution based on the most ideal intentions we can find in the depths of our collective human soul. In those depths, we are in unity with all being.

It is time for us to leave such a mind-stretching perspective and build the best rational visible foundations we can to map our potential future. At some level, making the transition from our full human potential to a discussion of domain mapping momentarily throws us off balance. The shift from ideal intentions to mapping the successful growth of businesses and other enterprises seems, at first, to be an abrupt change. Yet all human activity influences evolution and what and how we learn to be. We can show that business, in particular, has been a strong force in driving evolution. There is nothing to stop the world domain of business from helping to lead the conscious, creative, collaborative, compassionate evolution of humanity.

The people of the world enjoy an unprecedented level of personal freedom sponsored in part by the technological breakthroughs of the information age. Information is power. Making it readily available worldwide through media such as print, radio, television, and the Internet has changed the power dynamic of the world.

From any vantage point, personal to organizational, national to global, we have accelerated into another major transformation of our species. The end of South African apartheid, the Berlin Wall, and the Soviet Union are all unexpected events exemplary of evolutionary change. All change has accelerated to become evolutionary change for better or worse. We now move our discussion into how I created the METAMATRIX® domain map and how you can use it to aid your becoming a CEO. No matter what your field of endeavor, you can come to see and realize that evolution is the only business.

6

Evolutionary Bridge Building

The work of conscious evolution as our only business and of creating a new conscious renaissance is so lofty and abstract that it cries out for a forward-to-nature platform from which to build. The work requires a thinking foundation that chief evolutionary officers (CEOs) need to create. Learning to create a domain map is the best forward-to-basics way to consciously evolve that we, as authors, know.

In Chapter 5 Gus recounts the history to date of human evolution set in a METAMATRIX® map. In later parts of this book, we discuss our prediction for the future of evolutionary life. As we conclude this first part of the book, I provide an overview of domain mapping, which I see as a leading evolutionary act that will help determine our healthy future together.

Domain mapping is the development of a master plan for an entire industry or realm of work and creation. By studying a domain, set in a METAMATRIX®, we can understand how far the domain has evolved. We can then use the cyclical growth characteristics of the current and future stages to predict how future growth and evolution will occur. This capability to envision and depict future growth is an important asset to any CEO intent on leading conscious evolution. Figure 6–1 is an example of the central dynamics of gather, repeat, share, and transform in a domain map for the food industry.

We can create a domain map for any industry; the food industry is an example used in this book. What all domain maps have in common is their use of the dynamics of the METAMATRIX® growth stages

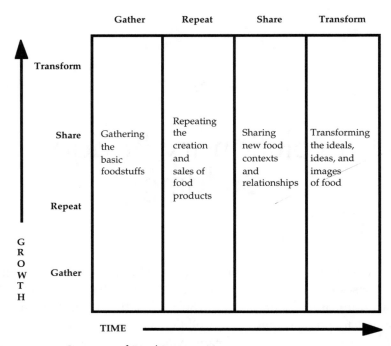

Figure 6–1   *Overview of Food Domain Map*

of gathering, repeating, sharing, and transforming to interpret past growth and predict future success and failure. Each domain map is individual to its industry. By basing each map in the current realities of the industry and using that basis to predict the future, we are assured of mapping from grounded reality through to highest future potential.

In the next part of this book, we provide the details of domain mapping and examples. To give you an overview understanding of domain mapping here, we include a four-column version to show the fundamental structure of a domain map of food in Figure 6–1. The main point to remember in looking at Figure 6–1 is that the four stages apply the dynamics of gathering, repeating, sharing, and transforming in analyzing the current activities within a domain. In Part II we will provide the details of domain mapping and give an example of a completed map.

EVOLUTIONARY CONTEXT FOR DOMAIN MAPPING

All human endeavors happen in the context of human evolution. That is just as true for the creation and growth of an industry as it is for any other area of evolution. By putting both the map of human evolution and domain mapping into the process-pattern of the METAMATRIX®, we can see how human evolution provides a broad and meaningful context for domain mapping. Appropriately placed in the human evolution map, domain mapping is located in the information age at R_s, as shown in Figure 6–2. By placing domain mapping at the site of our current evolution as humans in the information age, we indicate that the business environment is influenced by the same set of dynamics as all other current endeavors.

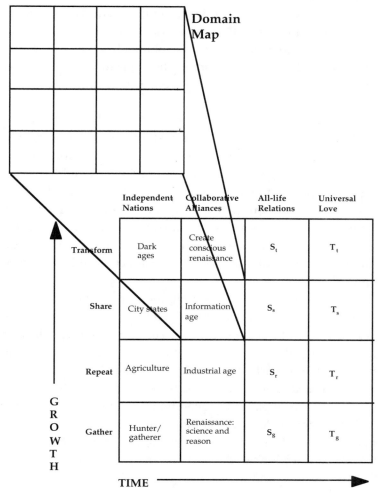

Figure 6–2 *Domain Map Set in Map of Human Evolution*

In addition to being a method for predicting the growth and profitable future of enterprises, domain mapping connects all enterprises, including businesses, in the broader process of human evolution. That is why we set forth our ideal intentions of evolution as the only business and life as the only customer.

BUSINESS LEADING EVOLUTION

The reason that the field of business holds such a vital interest for me is that in creating and serving markets, business is a prime force for leading us along the evolutionary, or devolutionary, path. That is, business has an enormous impact, both good and bad, on the evolution of life. To date, the contribution of business to evolution has been a by-product. With the advent of the CEO, we foresee the opportunity for business to take an active role in conscious evolution. The potential for positive, conscious evolution is enormous.

Gus has been discussing his philosophy and life's work and his study of general periodicity and transformational growth, which resulted in his creating the METAMATRIX®. I have focused more on the practical side, explaining how general periodicity and transformational growth relate to the working dynamics of the METAMATRIX®. I also have offered a brief resume so that you can understand my interest in domain mapping as a business application. Our intention is that the two threads of this book complement each other and stimulate your thinking about evolution as both an abstraction and as a practical, day-to-day reality.

There is, however, a stronger unifying force in the subject of this book that makes the writing of it compelling for us. The force is portrayed in the map of human evolution. The story the map tells is that we are all creating the evolutionary path for our species and, by implication, for all life on earth. Our participation is either implicit or conscious and explicit. The result is for better or worse. The important point is that we are all players in evolution, consciously or otherwise.

When we locate domain mapping within the map of human evolution, we are in effect saying that business, too, impacts the evolution of our species. If we look to the past and the present, we can see both positive and negative influences on evolution. For example, the entire transportation industry, including automobiles, trains, planes, and even space flight, has had an enormous impact on every aspect of our daily lives. We now have a freedom of movement that was unimaginable at the beginning of this century. Using this freedom of movement, we have expanded and changed our view of earth and see it now as the one world it really is. Phrases like "the western world" sound very parochial and dated. Perhaps nothing has done more to heighten our sense of the family of humankind, though, than the views of earth from space. These images have added both reality and awe to our understanding of the shared sense of being global citizens.

We are increasingly aware of the devolutionary impact of industry on our environment and our species. Industrial waste has caused areas of toxic pollution. Although we know the short-term results of such fouling of our environment, such as increased cancer rates among inhabitants of those areas, we are slow to determine the long-term impacts, such as potential changes to the gene pool. For example, the news media have reported on studies of mutations and extinction of frog species worldwide. Frogs are interesting subjects because their reproductive cycles are short, allowing alterations of the gene pool to become visible much more rapidly than among humans. Frogs also are more environmentally sensitive than most animals and expose themselves to pollutants in both the water and the air. They may be for modern life the warning signal that canaries used to be for miners, and they now are giving a strong signal of environmental problems.

The power of industry to enhance our lives is great. For example, the introduction of personal computers and the Internet has made a growing number of the world's population active participants in the information age. This power of industry to influence our lives and indeed all life is why, as we look at the use of domain maps to build the business enterprises of the future, we issue a call to leaders to become CEOs whose conscious intent, besides building a healthy bottom line in an annual report, is to help humanity and all life evolve to a healthy future.

GOOD BUSINESS EQUATION

In the end, success depends on the ability of an enterprise to learn that evolution is the only business. The equation of evolution and business is indeed bidirectional. The ability of a business to grow and reinvent itself is essential to long-term success. On the other hand, an enterprise that takes on as its business participation in the conscious evolution of our species and life on earth is conducting its affairs at the level with the highest potential for abundant profit, monetary and otherwise.

Anyone with business experience knows intuitively that growth and change are integral parts of the business process. George Land and Beth Jarman (1992) give a very well-reasoned explanation of the link between change and business success in terms of transformational growth in their book *Breakpoint and Beyond*. Business school curricula are filled with courses on change management to prepare future leaders for their roles as the implementers of change. Change is, after all, evolution and a fundamental of business. Managing that change is the job of chief executive officers and other leaders.

Chief evolutionary officers, on the other hand, look at the equation of evolution and business from a different perspective. CEOs see conscious evolution as the real end and ideal intention of all human endeavors, including business. Business becomes the means to achieving the ideal. Business is uniquely situated to be an agent of change and driver of evolution because it holds and integrates the intellectual and monetary resources and the entrepreneurial energy to turn visions into reality. When President Kennedy caught our imaginations with his vision of a man on the moon, American science and business built the entire space industry to make that vision a reality. The success of that reality, most often expressed in a view of our blue planet from space, is now an image shared across humanity.

Somehow in our current age we may have allowed ourselves to believe that doing well and doing good are antithetical. Our point in giving CEOs the tools of domain mapping is to show that doing well financially and doing good for life and the community are the same thing, that evolution is the only business.

POWER OF PREDICTION

A key to the use of any METAMATRIX® application, including domain mapping, is to think about and rigorously apply dynamics of the four stages of gathering, repeating, sharing, and transforming. With practice, four-phase progressions become easy. Table 6–1 provides a few examples.

As we look across the phases in Table 6–1, we get a sense of building toward the future. It is a growth force captured in the dynamic sequence of gather, repeat, share, and transform. With this growth force, domain mapping provides a frame for innovative interpretation of the current realities of an area of endeavor. It provides the foundation for expressing ideal intention of the future. That is, prediction is possible with evolutionary dynamics.

Prediction is the key to planning a successful future. With the map of human evolution and domain mapping, CEOs have the broadest possible vantage point from which to envision and plan the future. From there it is possible to predict the needs of humanity and to grow the mapped domain in a direction that meets those needs. Foreseeing the future needs of humanity and creating a vision for meeting those needs in harmony with all life is our definition of ideal intention or service to life.

Service to life is what we mean when we say that life is the only customer. By anticipating humanity's needs, a CEO can create a force that helps to lead us to our next stage of evolution. The success of the enterprise and life itself both are enhanced and become mutually enhancing. That is why, in the next part of this book, we examine the ideal intention that life is the only customer as we learn more about mapping domains, examine the process for creating a domain map, and look in detail at an example of a completed domain map.

Table 6–1 *Gather, Repeat, Share, and Transform Progressions*

Gather	Repeat	Share	Transform
Intend	Design	Build	Become
Analyze	Replicate	Redesign	Evoke
Resource	Product	Service	Value
Conscious	Creative	Collaborative	Compassionate
Physical	Mental	Emotional	Spiritual

Part II

Life Is the Only Customer

This is the first time in the history of our species that we have awakened to the realization that if our endeavors and enterprises are not life enhancing, they are killing us. The level of toxicity in our physical and social environment has risen steadily in recent decades, calling us to spend increasing time and thought on our health and self-protection. It is time to seek a successful coevolutionary agenda with life itself. It is time to offer life our most careful, creative, and reverent service. In all our getting and spending, if we do not transform our intentions and motives to enhance and protect and secure the sanctity of life, we will perish in the excesses and carelessness of our greed. This book will help you make the case to everyone's and everything's mutual benefit that life is the only customer.

7

Creating the METAMATRIX®
Domain Map

As Sue has said, a centerpiece thinking tool that we bring to assist your self-development as a chief evolutionary officer (CEO) is the use of the general periodic stages of transformational growth and evolution in the METAMATRIX® domain map. This mapping method provides the necessary thinking power of a very broad overview of your whole domain of creation within the context of our human species' global development. Learning to map your domain of creative work helps you to find your most evolutionary ideal intention of service to life. Here is some further rationale for use of domain maps and the story of how I developed this mapping process.

We know that evolution helps life itself grow toward forms more complex, more highly ordered, and in the case of humans, with more potential influence on all life. Service to life is central to the dynamics of evolution. We are now learning that service to all life is critical to the survival of our own human species and to evolutionary fulfillment. It is devolving behavior to disregard lives throughout nature and expect human life to thrive. If we think of evolution on earth as nature's business venture, life is its only customer.

In the web of nature, evolution serves all lives in the balance and harmony of their regenerative interaction and growth. Discovering the complexity of the interrelations of life in the study of ecology bears this out and reaffirms the similar ancient wisdom of indigenous cultures. For a CEO seeking to conduct the business of healthy evolution, it is fitting to reach for the ideal intention that life is the only customer.

DOMAIN MAPPING

In the creation of METAMATRIX® domain mapping, this realization about life as the only customer emerged early on. I discovered from the first domain mapping of the health and nutrition initiatives in the food industry that companies that evolved themselves farthest in service to the health and nutrition of their customers did far better in their earnings and strategic business advancement. Their evolutionary position and the advantage of profoundly serving the lives of their customers was clear to see on those first domain maps.

The story of the creation of domain mapping is again a story of visual synthesis. After I had developed the sixteen-square METAMA-TRIX®, I began to use it to consider the development of human learning and communication with Marilyn Norris, a colleague working at JC Penney. I also began work on mapping both human individual maturation and evolution of the human species and began to see the relationship between individuals and our species as special cases of the overarching pattern of general periodic, transformative growth. Each helps to evolve the other in the process of passing through the same stages of creative dynamics.

The life development story of an individual, called *ontogeny,* shares the same sequence of dynamic stages as the life evolution story of the species, called *phylogeny.* The long-sought-after theory that ontogeny repeats and advances the patterns of phylogeny is true, and so is the reverse that phylogeny repeats and advances ontogeny. The power and usefulness of this relationship for CEOs planning evolutionary learning is limitless.

As the work proceeded, a friend working at Harvard introduced me to the map of the whole domain of the information business created by the Program on Information Resources Policy. Their map presented on one page all the kinds of media and machinery and services that make up the entire information business domain. The mapmakers had used two axes of meaning, products to services vertically and form to substance horizontally on a rectangle to place everything from paper to professional services in its appropriate place. With this elegantly simple map of a whole domain they could chart various companies in the information business over time as they undertook new initiatives and roles with the technologies and services that make up the domain.

Seeing this map and its use to chart change over time was a great inspiration to me. The sixteen-square METAMATRIX® adds development over time, stage after stage up each column and across the columns in the gather, repeat, share, transform (GRST) sequence. I began to imagine how the two kinds of maps might be combined so that the METAMATRIX® showed the developmental sequence within the domain and thereby the ability to depict the evolution of the domain as a whole. The METAMATRIX® also could show the relative evolutionary positions and activities of the actors who created the domain. Seeking that relative position in the sixteen-square sequence turned out to be an extremely important capability for any ideal of strategic planning and for the definition of ideal intentions for growth in a domain. Knowing the location of the domain leaders in their fundamental creative dynamics and intentions is illuminating, inspiring, and challenging. Furthermore, use of the METAMATRIX® and its spiral as a domain map created discoveries of new potential for expanding the domain itself or even for creating new combinations of actors in whole new domains of endeavor. This type of creative, collaborative thinking is crucial to the evolutionary process of finding new services and markets for the customer of life itself.

HEALTH AND NUTRITION: THE FIRST DOMAIN

The first two ideal intentions emerged from my very first professional use of domain mapping. The work was for the Pillsbury Company in 1986. After reading five years of annual reports and other materials from each of seven large food companies to analyze and assess their activity in health and nutrition products and programs, I created an underlying domain map of the food industry (Figure 7–1).

I placed the stories of each company's health and nutrition initiatives (Figure 7–2) in each of the sixteen squares with their different dynamics, from the basic growing or gathering of foodstuffs at G_g to the transformation of the ideas, images, and ideals of food at T_t.

It became clear from the stories and the attendant earnings figures that the companies that went farthest in the sharing work of creat-

		Gather	Repeat	Share	Transform
↑	**Transform**	Value food and create new products	Value product and create new contexts and relationships	Value context and create new food ideals and images	Value ideal intentions, ideas, images; create new transcendent food concepts
	Share	Collect and distribute	Distribute and sell	Share and integrate relationships	Synthesize and invent new integrations and intentions
	Repeat	Cultivate and harvest	Process— manufacture and practice	Repeat and develop context and relationships	Actualize and practice ideals
G R O W T H	**Gather**	Plant and grow and catch	Prepare product and process	Prepare and form sharing context	Gather and formulate ideals, ideas, and images

TIME/SPACE ⟶

Figure 7–1 *Original Domain Map of the Food Industry*

		Gather	Repeat	Share	Transform
G R O W T H	**Transform**	Biotechnology Plant genetics New product creation Old product modification	International market development Statement of new market characteristics	Top executive Leadership; New eorporate image NCI-joint health promotion	
	Share		Consumer studies Newsletters Pamphlets Consumer information	Health and nutrition symposia R&D on fiber-cholesterol relationship 800 line Speaker advocate Nutrition consumer diet plan	Corporate culture Social invention and innovation
	Repeat		Nutrition computer database on all products Health and nutrition labeling	Restaurant menu changes and promotion	Public health and nutrition programs Corporate wellness and fitness programs
	Gather	Patent on hydroponic farming	Irradiation research Patent - process Texture fresh Whole grain Flake process New products Modified products	Food companies Exercise companies Medical companies	TV ads Nutrition policy Home Videos

TIME/SPACE ➤

Figure 7–2 *Completed Domain Map of the Food Industry*

ing new health-related contexts and relationships in business and those that consciously changed and transformed their purpose and identity to focus on health clearly dominated. In their depth of service and breadth of product offerings, those companies gained the highest percentage of earnings in the emerging market where profits far exceed the overall earnings in the food industry at large. These evolutionary leading companies stretched the food industry domain to include buying restaurant chains for the ability to change menus toward health and even buying exercise equipment companies.

One leader evolved beyond the domain itself to conduct research on indigenous grains in countries all over the world to be able to serve humanity in the case of shortages of animal and fish protein. That same company, Kellogg, teamed with the National Cancer Institute and the Food and Drug Administration to promote the value of bran in the prevention of intestinal cancer. Collaboration with medical science and government agencies for the enhancement of public, national, and global health expands into a whole new domain of higher service to life. These self-evolved companies proved by how well they earned in leading the public good that evolution is good business.

Because failure to lead or even follow the leaders had the reverse effect on earnings and stature with the public, it became clear that growing in service to life is a market necessity. By the same token, we have come full circle to the ideal intention that evolution is the only business. It is because people have the creature wisdom to eat as well as possible to enhance their lives that with their wisdom they continuously teach us that life is the only customer.

Both these ideal intentions are a stretch and a reach way beyond business as usual. Yet they are essential values and codes of behavior for CEOs because of our stated principle of seeking to work with and for evolution and life. In Chapter 11, I consider the guiding values and attributes of the CEO and the work of creating conscious renaissance. In Chapters 8 through 10, Sue discusses in detail how to develop domain maps and provides an example. The thinking work will be well worth your effort.

8

Domain Mapping

Every enterprise exists within a larger domain. Whether you are the leader of a for-profit business or of a nonprofit institution, other organizations are doing work that is similar to the work of your enterprise. These other organizations can be your competitors, other institutions with which you have collaborative relationships, or simply groups with parallel functions. The collection of similar enterprises makes up a *domain*. Whether the relation between these enterprises is competitive, symbiotic, or unconscious, understanding what others in a domain are doing adds to the richness of your perception of the world and its trends. This creative perception gives you an evolutionary advantage to be a leader and lead your domain.

Bringing a knowledge and appreciation of the dynamics of growth and evolution to an understanding of your domain provides a powerful method of analysis and an easily shared thinking tool. By categorizing other products and services within the domain in terms of these evolutionary dynamics, you can gain a strong sense for what others are doing to grow their enterprises. You can also see gaps that provide near-term opportunities and creative niches. Most important, however, you can start to ask the questions that will lead to an evolutionary re-creation of your enterprise that is both consistent and collaborative with nature's success stages and with humanity's striving for progress. This striving is both good evolution and good business for all types of enterprises.

We use the four main stages of the METAMATRIX® to examine four major aspects of a domain (Figure 8–1). The first stage focuses on

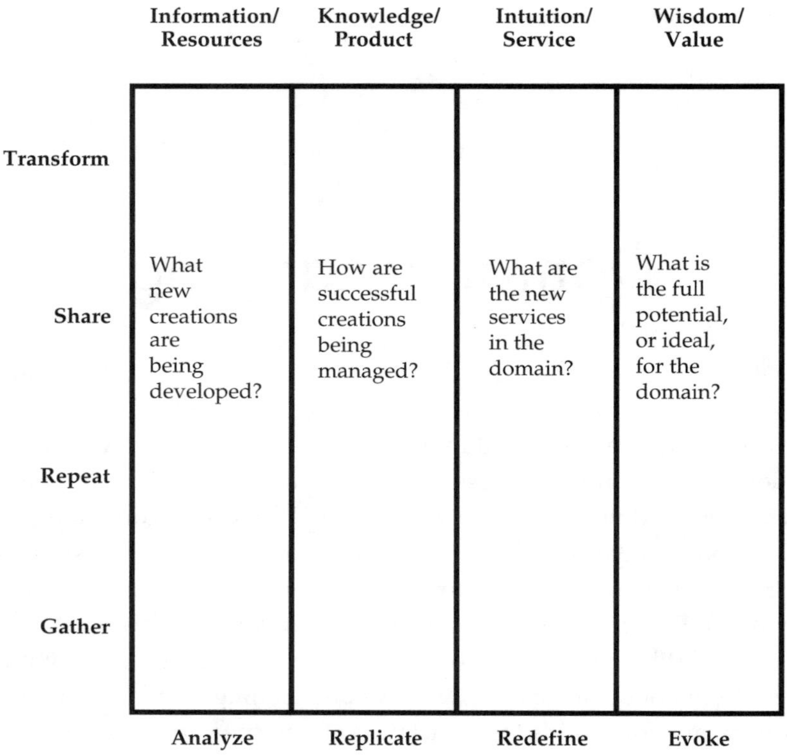

	Information/ Resources	Knowledge/ Product	Intuition/ Service	Wisdom/ Value
Transform				
Share	What new creations are being developed?	How are successful creations being managed?	What are the new services in the domain?	What is the full potential, or ideal, for the domain?
Repeat				
Gather				
	Analyze	**Replicate**	**Redefine**	**Evoke**

Analyze: Analysis of developing creations
Replicate: Analysis of successful creations
Redefine: Analysis of creations integrating services to serve
    society
Evoke: Analysis of the domain's future potential and new
    identity to evolve common well-being

Figure 8–1   *Overview of Domain Map*

emerging creations (products, processes, and ideas) that will become new trend-setting offerings in the domain. In the second stage, we look at currently successful creations to gain a sense of the domain's repeated multiplicity, that is, its current bread and butter. The third stage examines creations that are being redefined as services and new creative contexts to broaden participation through the integration of new and different relationships. In the fourth stage, we look at the highest potential of the domain to gain an ideal view of how the domain can connect with and contribute to the evolution of humanity by serving life as the primary customer.

In creating a domain map, you should look at the activities of all major participants in the domain in each of the four stages. Depending on your knowledge of the domain in question, you may easily identify the appropriate activities for each participant in the domain, or you may need to do additional research. If you need to do additional research, public documents, such as annual reports and articles in the news media, provide useful information.

Later in this chapter, I discuss in detail the sorting, categorization, and placement of various activities on a domain map. Before I do that, however, let's look more closely at the dynamics in action in a domain map.

DYNAMICS OF THE INFORMATION AGE

It is important to remember that domain mapping occurs in the here and now of the information age at R_s on the map of human evolution (see Figure 8–1). The primary dynamic of this stage is replication, the making, repeating, and promoting of many products or services. The secondary dynamic, however, is sharing because of its emphasis on the integration of differences. Because domain mapping is done in the information age of human evolution, we can expect to see the primary and secondary dynamics permeate this discussion of domain mapping.

A good example of an enterprise with strong R_s behavior is the U.S. Postal Service. The postal service is now supplementing its primary role as mail carrier with an effort to sell stamps to collectors. To expand its market, the postal service has made the shift from seeing stamps as a currency with which we purchase its mail services to being objects of desire for collectors. Post offices around the country notify potential collectors of new stamps before they become available. The postal service is selling more of its product (stamps) by integrating differences that appeal to collectors as well as to its traditional patrons. The price of the stamp or sheet of stamps is the same for a collector as for someone with a letter to mail. Yet the postal service does not have the expense of delivering the letter or package for the collector.

We have added some new column labels to the four vertical stages of the METAMATRIX® in Figure 8–1 to tailor it to the rigors of domain mapping and to make the dynamics more apparent. The labels on the rows retain the expression of gather, repeat, share, and transform (GRST) to emphasize the isomorphic (identical in process and structure) aspect of all maps. The column headings are tailored to both domain mapping and our time in the information age. These headings are consistent with the dynamics of the respective gather, repeat, share, or transform stages in which they appear, as shown in Table 8–1.

The headings are designed to make the context for the dynamics of gather, repeat, share, transform more apparent as we apply them in the domain mapping process.

The first stage of a domain map focuses on *gathering* the basic building blocks in the form of physical resources, new processes, and new information or ideas to produce the prototype of a new creation. At each step of the first stage (G_g through G_t) in the domain map, we assess the new creations of colleagues and competitors in our domain and track their progress or failure in the gather stage.

In the *repeat* stage, we describe the activities needed to replicate a successful creation. Our focus is on activities that produce and promote creations in volume. At each step of the second stage (R_g through R_t) in the domain map, we assess the action taken by others in our domain to proliferate their creations in their particular marketplace or area of service.

In the *share* stage, we describe the introduction of new services or the reworking of existing products to reinvent them as services. The reinvention of products as services is both a significant and substantial change for the enterprise because it represents a shift in the work of the enterprise and its underlying motivation for existing. It is also an opportunity for abundant profit in financial and life-serving terms because it broadens the potential market and service area in an all-

Table 8–1   *Four Columns of Domain Mapping*

Gather	Repeat	Share	Transform
Information	Knowledge	Intuition	Wisdom
Resource	Product	Service	Value
Analyze	Replicate	Redefine	Evoke

inclusive way. The shift to services greatly widens and deepens the pool of potential participants by redefining customers to include those not previously viewed as potential customers and to include customers who are conscious collaborators in well-being. It is another instance in which evolution is good business and life is the best customer and conscious collaborator.

At each of the four steps in the third stage (S_g through S_t), we use words that come more from our creative side than from our rational side. We emphasize intuition, service, and redefinition. In the next section, Differentiating Products from Services, we discuss the shift from product to service and its impact on enterprises and life in general.

In the *transform* stage, we use words to describe the emergence of the domain at a new, higher order to serve life. The purpose of the enterprise becomes evoking new value-based services that meet the basic needs of humanity and our environment. This wise view of a domain's highest potential purpose is very important. It fills our vision of the domain's potential with hope and energy to create what we would otherwise not foresee as possible. It is the magnet to pull forth our dreams. We do not expect to see a great deal of domain activity in the transform stages (nor should we preclude the possibility of finding any). We can, however, use the transform stage to energize our view of the future for expansion and evolution in our domain and for those we serve.

DIFFERENTIATING PRODUCTS FROM SERVICES

As we work our way across a domain map, the shift from product to service is a very important evolutionary leap both conceptually and in terms of profit potential, that is, for both financial reward and life usefulness. Yet it is not always easy to differentiate a product from a service. For example, we all know about pizza delivery services. Are they really a service, or are they simply a way to sell more pizzas through a new sales channel? Let's amplify the definitions of the words *product* and *service* to clear up this ambiguity:

- A *product* is something we package and sell. It can be a physical object, such as a ballpoint pen, or an intellectual product, such as a personal skills assessment tool. The product includes its manufacturing and distribution or delivery systems. The product can be mass manufactured and sold in retail outlets around the world, or it can be taught in classrooms to small groups of students. In either case, the goal with a product is always to sell more, to manufacture more pens and to teach more classes. Other examples of products are software packages and consulting contracts with large corporations to reengineer their enterprises. Products from pizza to consulting on corporate reengineering can embody services, but the motivation for the service is to sell more product. That underlying motivation is the key differentiator.

- A *service* has as its goal the creation of social change. A service promotes evolution and healthy life in support of the first two ideal intentions—that evolution is the only business and life is the only customer. A service is much more than an activity designed to make a product more desirable.

What follows are two examples of services by our definition: one in the food industry and the other in the organizational consulting business.

The food industry is highly product based. A tour of your local supermarket, which has rows and rows of shelves containing every imaginable food product, drives home this product orientation in the food domain. Some food companies, however, have made the shift to providing services that promote change through educating people about the link between food and health.

By forming alliances with nonprofit institutions such as the American Heart Association, some food companies are transforming themselves into nutrition and health companies. The result of these alliances is a strong effort to teach people about a healthful diet. Food then becomes a pathway to health and is more than just another product to consume. Selling people good nutrition and health is a service in support of life as the best, long-term customer.

Within the domain of organizational-change consulting, we can find a wide array of tools, instruments, and philosophies. Each of these is designed to help the consultant produce change in a client's enterprise. Typically these change programs support a range of activities from individual development to team development and creation of learning organizations. In this particular example, it is the motivation

behind the change program within the company that is key to determining whether consulting is a product or a service.

If the motivation for building individual, team, and organizational learning skills is to streamline the enterprise for the purpose of
producing more products more efficiently and at lower cost, then the
consulting work to accomplish this change is a product. The tools of
change are oriented toward process reengineering and replication and
not toward the process of cultural evolutionary development and maturation.

If the motivation for building individual, team, and organizational learning skills is to honor and evoke the knowledge, intelligence,
and creativity that people, both individually and in groups, bring to
their work, then the consulting work is an evolutionary service. The
tools of change are oriented toward changing the way in which people
work with each other to produce an integration of differences that
educes deeper qualities of what it means to be human.

We are not advocating that enterprises abandon their bread-and-
butter products to create a new evolutionary future. One aspect of the
METAMATRIX® implicit in our discussions so far is that the four
stages of gather, repeat, share, and transform are cumulative. Enterprises can carry their products forward into their new service-oriented
stage.

Certainly, food companies, while teaching us about health and
nutrition will continue to sell their products. In fact, teaching health
and nutrition creates a stronger market for health-oriented food products, and the additional profit from these products more than pays for
the teaching. The point is that the profit is mutual; customers and the
company benefit. A shift to services brings with it the potential of
greatly widening and deepening market share and increasing profits in
for-profit enterprises just as an expansion of services increases the
opportunity for funding and clients in a nonprofit enterprise.

Companies that provide evolutionary service should expect to
create greater financial profit as they broaden their customer base. Such
services both increase the opportunity for products and build relationships that increase customer loyalty. For example, when we study the
nutrition pyramid and the American Heart Association endorsement on
our box of morning cereal, we learn that the company that makes the
cereal cares about our health. Once we know that a particular company

cares about our health, we are likely to look for other similarly healthful products from that company and spend a greater share of our earnings on that company's products.

The underlying motivation then is the key to differentiating a product from a service. If our goal is to replicate and promote our product to broader markets and areas of service, we are in the product business even though our product may include supporting services. If our goal is to help people evolve to leading better, healthier lives, we are in the service business, even if we sell products. We make the differentiation on the basis of motivation and ideal intention.

The evolutionary shift from product to service is huge. It means changing from the mentality of multiplicity to a mindset built on relationships. Relationships, with their associated integration of differences, form the basis for effective social services and beneficial change. With productive relationships, the opportunity for an enterprise to increase its service area of influence and financial profit is great. The enterprise truly reinvents itself in a whole new context of potential.

This context of new potential is an evolutionary context. Although the effort the enterprise makes to reinvent itself is important, so too should be the profits it reaps for itself and generates for all its stakeholders. The new context provides a broader service area and richer opportunities for serving humankind and for being well compensated in return. This service context clearly demonstrates that evolution is good business for everyone from producer to collaborative health-wise customer and for all such evolving enterprises. Once again we assert that life is the only customer.

9

How to Map
a Domain

For me, this chapter is the meat and potatoes of our book. It is where
we describe how to use the METAMATRIX® as a tool for mapping
your domain. The stages of gather, repeat, share, and transform
(GRST) will guide our analysis of how the domain has progressed so
far and will give us insight into where it is going. This view into the
future, based on natural growth stages, is what gives the METAMA-
TRIX® and its users the power of prediction.

THE GENERIC DOMAIN MAP

To make the analysis of a domain easier to approach, we have created a
generic domain map. We have taken the four-stage domain map overview from Figure 8–1 and used its four columns titled resource, product, service, and value to create a more detailed and fractal version
containing the full sixteen sections. This level of greater detail provides
us with more information about the current domain and its future, as
shown in Figure 9–1.

Each of the four questions in the GRST stages has become a new
set of four questions related to the larger question. Each of the sixteen
questions in the more detailed map is based on the dynamics of gather,
repeat, share, and transform within its respective stage.

	Information/ Resources	Knowledge/ Product	Intuition/ Service	Wisdom/ Value
Transform	Will the new creation succeed? What form will it take to be repeated?	How might the creation integrate new services to achieve social change?	How do these services seek new value potential?	How does the created value serve the evolution of life?
Share	How is the new creation being popularized?	What are the new expansive connections channels and supports?	How do these relationships profit life?	What is the currency, the dynamic of sharing of the new value?
Repeat	What is the essential, repeatable element of its success?	How many? How often? Where?	What are the new repeatable relationships?	What is the enduring beneficial impact of new value manifestation?
Gather	What new creation is being developed?	What is the replication process? How does it work?	Who are new collaborative colleagues? What is new context?	What is the higher identity of the new value potential?
	Analyze	Replicate	Redefine	Evoke

Analyze: Analysis of developing creations
Replicate: Analysis of successful creations
Redefine: Analysis of creations integrating services to serve society
Evoke: Analysis of the domain's future potential and new identity to evolve common well-being

R_s

Human Evolution:
Information Age in R_s

Figure 9–1 *Generic Domain Map with Questions*

To create a map of your domain, you should follow these steps.

1. Identify the other enterprises in your domain.
2. Acquire as much information as possible about the enterprises through research, for example, by reading several years of annual reports for each participant to repeat their stories in GRST format.
3. Apply each of the sixteen questions to the activities of each enterprise and record significant answers in the appropriate

section of the map to integrate stories with the appropriate dynamic stages of the map.

4. Put your own enterprise in its appropriate place on the map and begin the creative process of imagining the future dynamics of the evolution of your enterprise

By answering these questions for all the members of your domain, you can create a thorough analysis of that domain and instantiate that analysis in a visual map to heighten awareness of the future with its trends and opportunities. Depending on your preference, there are three ways in which you can approach these questions. Each produces benefits but requires varying levels of time and effort on your part.

- You can read through the questions to gain a deeper understanding of domain mapping without crafting your responses to them. This is the approach I had in mind in describing the questions.
- You can do the detailed work to create your own map. Gus and I are available to help you with this process. Chapter 13 contains information on how to contact us.
- You can skip the questions all together and rely on the overview of domain mapping in the four-column form provided in Figure 8–1. This figure and the domain mapping example in Chapter 10 will provide you with a sufficient foundation for understanding domain mapping for the time being.

Regardless of the approach that suits you best, our intention is that the domain mapping process will help you look at your domain in a new and creative light.

QUESTIONS ON THE GENERIC DOMAIN MAP

As you look at various domain maps with us, it is important that we all feel the sense of growth and evolution that occurs within each of the four stages and across the stages. Each set of four questions is designed to build on that growth momentum within the stages. Let's take a minute to look at the questions individually, starting with the first question in the lower left of the domain map. We will consider them in groups of four, one group for each of the four stages.

The Gather Stage (Resources, Information, Analyze)

The gather stage is the stage of new beginnings. It contains the analysis of new products, processes, and ideas to assess them for potential use and salability. The questions in this stage are as follows.

What New Creation Is Being Developed? (G_g)   This is the question that starts the domain map. It is intended to identify new possibilities starting within your domain. Things to consider are new materials and raw resources being used, new processes under design, new information pertinent to the domain, and new ideas to be tested.

What Is the Essential, Repeatable Element of Its Success? (G_r)   For any of the possibilities identified with the answer to the first question to become a real product in the repeat stage, it must have a core aspect that repeatedly and consistently appeals to its potential customers or clients. The core aspect can be anything from a modification to a manufacturing process that will save money in mass production, or it can be a unique idea that could potentially spawn a whole new domain of enterprises. In any case, the possibility must have a core that appeals to potential customers if it is to become a success.

How Is the New Creation Being Popularized? (G_s)   A critical step for any creation is to tell its potential customers or clients about it. This is the communication or sharing of the product, process, or idea. Understanding how others in your domain are popularizing their creations is to learn about new relationships with customers and clients that will create demand for the new creation. One possible result of this sharing is to learn that people would like the creation if it were modified in some specific way.

Will the New Creation Succeed? What Form Will It Take to Be Repeated? (G_t)   Having looked at a creation, assessed its essential and repeatable element of success, and determined the method of popularization, we are now in a position (G_t) to decide whether the creation will ever succeed with customers. The possible answers here are yes, no, and yes with modifications. That is, the creation may be so well designed that there is an instant set of customers or clients for it, or it may be so far off the mark that it needs to be completely redesigned, starting at G_g again. The more likely case is that the creation will need some kind of modification so that its final form is both repeatable and desired by customers or clients. This determination is important because it will set the stage for the success or failure of the creation in the R stage.

The Repeat Stage (Product, Knowledge, Replicate)

The repeat state is the stage of new proliferation. It looks at volume issues for the creation, such as the replication process, the number created, and new channels. The questions in this stage are as follows.

What Is the Replication Process? How Does It Work? (R_g)   This is the question that looks at how the product is made. For tangible products, we look at the manufacturing process. For intellectual property and services, such as consulting, we look at how the knowledge is packaged for the client.

How Many? How Often? Where? (R_r)   In our current place in the information age, we judge the success of a creation by the demand for it. At this stage in our domain map, we look to see what the production volume is, how often the creation is produced and in how many places, and what the sales numbers are.

What Are the New Expansive Channels, Connections, and Supports? (R_s)   Once a creation has achieved success and volume, enterprises typically create new opportunities to continue the growth curve. Through the integration of differences (sharing), enterprises create new relationships and adapt creations to meet the needs of expanded numbers and kinds of customers and clients.

How Might the Creation Integrate New Services to Achieve Social Change? (R_t)   This section at the top of the repeat stage is a very real test point for every enterprise. Every enterprise must decide whether it will forge forward into the services area of the share and transform stages or stay in the product, process, and idea stages of gather and repeat through the continual introduction of new creations. Enterprises that decide to move forward on the evolutionary curve must start the work of transforming a product mentality into an evolutionary view to search out their unique opportunity for serving life as the customer. The purpose of this question is to look at how such a transformation might happen.

The Share Stage (Service, Intuition, Redefine)

The share stage is the stage of new meaning making through integration. It looks at the transformation of the old product line into a new service or set of services that foster evolutionary development through new relationships. The questions in this stage are as follows.

Who Are the New Collaborative Colleagues? What Are the New Settings or Contexts? (S_g)   Building new relationships that serve life is key to the transition from product to service. In addition, the collaborative quality of the relationships and contexts is essential to success. The service should benefit the providers (that is, the collaborative colleagues) as well as the intended clients and customers.

What Are the New Repeatable Relationships? (S_r)   Trusting, enduring relationships are key to delivering a consistently high-quality service. Understanding the relationships built among the clients and the collaborative colleagues will give us a good understanding of the basis for the success of the service.

How Do These Relationships Profit Life? (S_s)   A service produces social change that serves life. That evolution is the underlying motivation for the service. With this question, we want to find who in the domain is creating relationships that profit others as well as the profiting enterprise. Providing a service that benefits life as the customer must be the motivation for a share stage success.

How Do These Services Seek New Value Potential? (S_t)   The top of every stage is a key decision point for every enterprise. Our position here at S_t is no different. Will the enterprise continue providing beneficial services, or will it break out into the next stage to reach for the ideal vision it holds for its domain in service to life?

The Transform Stage (Value, Wisdom, Evoke)

This is the stage of transformation. In the transform stage we look for ways to evoke the full potential wisdom and value of a service to reach a higher-order meaning and benefit to life.

The answers to the questions posed in this section have the potential for positioning the enterprise for a breakout into a whole new domain of endeavor, as shown in Figure 9–2.

The METAMATRIX® set in a golden rectangle and evolving into a series of METAMATRIX®es along a spiral of increasing magnitude is the symbol we use for the transform stage.

What Is the Higher Identity of the New Value Potential? (T_g)   The values that an enterprise sees as ideal for its domain provide the path for its next evolutionary step after the sharing of beneficial services. Identifying and internalizing those values is the key step on which all transform stage activities build.

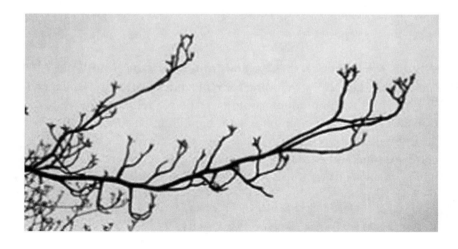

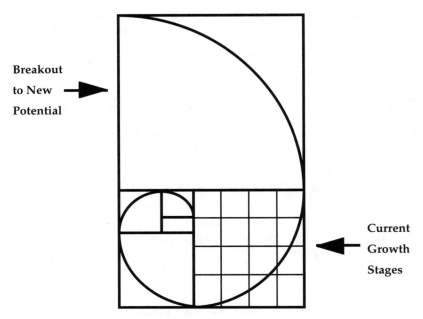

Breakout
to New
Potential

Current
Growth
Stages

Figure 9–2   *Transformation into New Domains*

What Is the Enduring Beneficial Impact of the New Value Manifestation? (T_r)   This question looks at how the new values are turned into concrete manifestations or actions. It addresses how people see the new values instantiated in ways that are both repeatable and reliable.

What Is the Currency, the Dynamic of Sharing the New Value? (T_s)
Money has been a long-standing form of compensation in human civilizations and will, no doubt, continue to be so. Yet as we move to the transform stage with its emphasis on shared human and life values, we also have the opportunity to seek out other currencies and forms of compensation and exchange of value. How can enterprises share their values to create other forms of life-enhancing abundance for others as well as themselves?

How Does the Created Value Serve the Evolution of Life? (T_t) We have placed our domain map in the information age of human evolution. Placing it there is acknowledgment that every enterprise, whether it is for profit or nonprofit, has a potential role in contributing to the evolution of life on earth. Creating a vision of that valuable service to evolution benefits the enterprise in two ways. That vision raises the optimism and the creativity for the enterprise's current activities by making common human values actionable within the daily lives of people working in the enterprise. The vision also defines the stepping stone for the next big step: enterprise evolution into conscious renaissance at R_t of the larger map of human evolution. This is where we find a truly new future for humanity. The power of such a vision to bring out the best in people is enormous.

Entering the transform stage of the human species (R_t) with vision and conviction brings a strong momentum that is extremely powerful. This transform stage is the last stage of industrial and information age evolution, as shown in Figure 9–3. Its position on the map of human evolution is critical to our survival. This location on the domain map (R_{st} on the map of human evolution) is where we go to position ourselves for the next great leap in human evolution to R_t. It is where chief evolutionary officers (CEOs) go to start creating a long-term future for their enterprises, all of humanity, and all of life based in the new relationships of conscious, collaborative, creative, compassionate (C4) communities. It is a place where pioneering and leadership set the stage for the next great surge in domain and species redefinition and growth.

We take a closer look at the new territory of R_t in Chapter 11. For now, suffice it to say that R_t is the doorway to the future. It poses many hard questions and gives us a view into great opportunity as humanity also positions itself for the cultural changes of evolving to the new macrostage of sharing. In effect, putting ourselves in R_t is truly a renaissance moment, as was humanity's previous position in G_t. Both G_t and R_t ask the questions that prepare us for the shift to the next stage on our map—evolutionary growth. The difference is that now we need all of humanity together to create a conscious renaissance of human evolution.

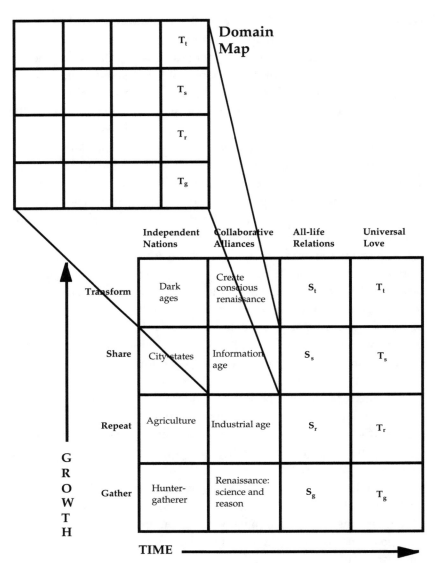

Figure 9–3 *Domain Map Transform Stage*

10

Sample Domain Map

Let's now take a look at a completed domain map for the food industry. The food industry is a good example of a domain because all of us, in one way or another, interact with it. To reinforce the connections between the generic map with its sixteen questions about domains in general and the domain map specific to the food industry, we have created a bridging map, shown in Figure 10–1. This map takes the generic questions of the domain map shown in Chapter 9 and restates them as areas of interest for the food industry in particular. It is important to understand that we are using the food industry to provide a sample of the possibilities that emerge from domain mapping. Our answers to the sixteen questions related to the food industry are not definitive and are meant to be thought provoking.

In generating the questions in Figure 10–1, we have made some exciting and potentially profitable translations of words such as *service* and *values* to more concrete words. *Service* becomes *health and nutrition*, and *values* become *life and environment*. Each translation is consistent with the dynamics of the map stage that contains the words. We look at these translations more closely in Figure 10–2, the food industry domain map.

For the moment, though, it is important to understand that the highly significant transitions that occur from one stage to the next are driven by the dynamics of the respective stages. Domains have made these shifts in the past, are making them now, and have the potential to do so in the future. Still, creating the vision of the future is hard work that requires us to use our own creativity. Drawing on the natural

	What new creations are being developed?	How are successful creations being managed?	What are the new services in the domain?	What is the full potential or ideal for the domain?
Transform	What form will new food products take?	How does the product create health and nutrition through relationships?	What can the new ideals and values of food become?	How does the created value promote evolution of life?
Share	How is food being collected and distributed?	What are the connections, channels and supports to sell and distribute?	How can collaborators tell people about health and nutrition?	How can life support become an international movement?
Repeat	What are the new ways of cultivating and harvesting?	What is the volume, frequency, and location of processing?	What are the new repeatable health and nutrition relationships?	What is being done to support environment and life?
Gather	What are the new ways of planting, growing, and catching?	How are food products being prepared and processed?	Who are the new colleagues and contexts in creating health and nutrition?	How can health expand to include environment and life?
	Analyze	Replicate	Redefine	Evoke

Analyze: Analysis of developing creations
Replicate: Analysis of successful creations
Redefine: Analysis of creations integrating services to serve society
Evoke: Analysis of the domain's future potential and new identity to evolve common well-being

R_s

Human Evolution: Information Age in R_s

Figure 10–1 *Domain Map with Food Industry Questions*

order creativity of the METAMATRIX® guides us in this work and helps to enhance and stretch our thinking.

Figure 10–2 is the sample domain map of the food industry. In creating this map, we gathered public information such as annual reports, used our own experiences with the food industry, and looked at advertising placed by the food industry. We then placed some of the more important examples of our findings in the METAMATRIX®.

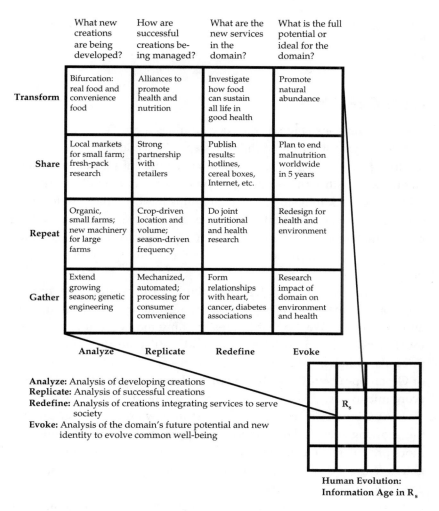

	What new creations are being developed?	How are successful creations be-ing managed?	What are the new services in the domain?	What is the full potential or ideal for the domain?
Transform	Bifurcation: real food and convenience food	Alliances to promote health and nutrition	Investigate how food can sustain all life in good health	Promote natural abundance
Share	Local markets for small farm; fresh-pack research	Strong partnership with retailers	Publish results: hotlines, cereal boxes, Internet, etc.	Plan to end malnutrition worldwide in 5 years
Repeat	Organic, small farms; new machinery for large farms	Crop-driven location and volume; season-driven frequency	Do joint nutritional and health research	Redesign for health and environment
Gather	Extend growing season; genetic engineering	Mechanized, automated; processing for consumer comvenience	Form relationships with heart, cancer, diabetes associations	Research impact of domain on environment and health
	Analyze	**Replicate**	**Redefine**	**Evoke**

Analyze: Analysis of developing creations
Replicate: Analysis of successful creations
Redefine: Analysis of creations integrating services to serve
   society
Evoke: Analysis of the domain's future potential and new
   identity to evolve common well-being

R_s

**Human Evolution:
Information Age in R$_s$**

Figure 10–2 *Sample Domain Map of the Food Industry*

As with all other domains, the food industry finds itself at repeating-share (R_s) on the map of human evolution. That is, it carries an emphasis on processing and manufacturing from the industrial age, is at present in the information age, and looks to a future in collaborative alliances at the top of the R stage and then to all-life relations in the S stage. Repeating and sharing are the primary and secondary dynamics, respectively. We now take a closer look at the four stages of the food industry domain map in Figure 10–2 and see how the dynamics play out.

NEW CREATIONS

The new creations stage of the food domain map (G_g) is its research and development, or gathering (G), stage. As we look at the activities occurring in this stage, we see two major types of participants: large enterprises (both farmers and food processors) and small enterprises. As we look back in history, we see that this has been the case for quite some time. We also see that the small enterprise was on the scene long before the larger ones were. Right now, in the information age, however, the large enterprises prevail over the domain, particularly in financial terms.

We include small enterprises (both farmers and food processors) on the map because of the growing interest in fresh, organic, and local foods. We see that interest gaining momentum for environmental, health, and social reasons and anticipate that small enterprises, or collaboratives of small enterprises, such as Cabot Creamery or Ocean Spray, will rapidly become or have already become leading economic forces.

At G_g we also see a great interest in new creations that prolong the growing season. For example, new processes and techniques for more productive and tastier hydroponic vegetables are under investigation. Newly designed greenhouses extend the growing season and ease gardening chores. Both small and large farmers benefit from methods for extending the growing season and are contributing to the creation of the technology that makes it possible. Here in Vermont, for example, from April through December we can purchase locally grown, organic tomatoes that have great flavor, texture, and color. That is a nine-month growing season rather than a four-month growing season and an appealing increase in the opportunity for profits.

We also see a number of activities by large enterprises to make produce more adaptable to the rigors of automatic harvesting and to have longer shelf lives. This type of research is primarily focused on reducing costs and waste in volume foods handled by large growers and producers.

Moving up the stage to G_r, we start to see a stronger split in the interests of smaller enterprises and larger ones. Smaller farmers work to learn more about sustainable farming that does not corrode the land and that will serve future generations. They develop new techniques to bring organically grown produce to local markets. Larger farmers test new methods of high-volume growing, such as mechanization, to bring quality products to consumers at the lowest possible cost. Both of the efforts are useful, and if we think of each type of enterprise in terms of stages of growth, the type of activities in which they engage make a great deal of sense.

Large enterprises have already completed at least one cycle through the gathering stage when they made the transition from being a start-up business to an established economic force. Collectively, the smaller enterprises working to establish sustainable farming as a new economic force are still gathering the methods, technology, and momentum that they need to succeed. Right now their niche is local markets and high-quality specialty foods, whereas larger enterprises have as their niche easily available, price competitive foods. In fact, these two markets (high end, high quality, and high volume, low price) are the markets that business schools classically advise entrepreneurs to pick.

The share section of the first stage (G_s) on the food domain map looks at issues of building markets. For the smaller enterprise, this means building relationships with local markets so that they will stock and feature local products. In some cases, it even means starting up a local farmers' market to create a place where local farmers and specialty food producers can interact with and sell to their consumers. For the larger enterprises, this means introducing new products and packaging into the supermarket chains. For example, we can see on the map where one large enterprise is experimenting with a special package that will help produce arrive to market fresh even if it has to travel long distances.

By the time we reach the top of the first stage (G_t) of our domain map, we can clearly see the emphasis the large enterprises place on consumer convenience and reduced costs while the smaller enterprises select specialty foods for their niche. Over time, we should expect to see these two trends recombine so that healthfulness and convenience become compatible traits in many foods and sustainable farming and high efficiency farming support each other. Another way of seeing the future is that the small enterprises will either become large individually or will collectively achieve critical mass, so that the quality and healthfulness of fresh, local food becomes a very important market force.

MANAGING SUCCESSFUL CREATIONS

In the first stage, we looked at research and development in the food domain. In this, the repeat stage, we look at how enterprises manage successful food products right now. This is the stage at which, for the present at least, large enterprises prevail. They have the money and capital resources to put in place technically sophisticated farms and processing plants so that replication benefits both the enterprise and the consumer. They are efficient enough to be profitable and still produce low-cost, desirable products both on the farm and in the processing plants. They also have the capital and know-how to produce a wide variety of convenience foods. With people around the world, particularly in the United States, working a record number of hours per year, the demand for convenience foods will continue to grow.

To a great extent in the R_r stage, nature's seasonal patterns determine the frequency of planting, though as mentioned earlier, research and experimentation to extend the growing seasons are underway and have produced results. So the questions of volume, frequency, and location apply more to food-processing plants and less to farmers. Processing plants tailored to a particular crop tend to be located where the crop is grown, for example, pineapples in Hawaii and oranges in Florida. Other processing plants handle a variety of produce (for example, a soup factory), and each enterprise has its own strategy for locating those plants. Because the raw produce to feed the processing plants is grown and available worldwide, market demand for the final product is the greatest influence on the volume and frequency of processing.

In the share section of the second stage (R_s) of the food domain map, we see a number of strong relationships that broaden the market for existing products. Food producers continue to maintain strong relationships with supermarkets but also look for new markets, such as restaurants and food services that supply restaurants, cafeterias, and institutions. Some even start their own restaurants to increase their markets. All of these activities build new relationships that increase product demand.

The top of the second stage (R_t) is a key decision point for all enterprises. The decision centers on whether the enterprise will remain a product company or make the commitment to become a service enterprise, that is, whether it will provide services that cause beneficial social change. As we look at the food domain, we see that some participants chose to remain in the product arena while others moved to services. Those who chose to move ahead did so by building their long-term visions as health and nutrition companies (rather than merely food producers) and building alliances with public institutions to receive public validation of their visions.

FOOD DOMAIN SERVICES

In the repeating stage of the food domain map, we looked at the operations of food enterprises selling successful products. In the sharing stage, we look at the relationships that some enterprises have built to become agents of community change as well as purveyors of products.

Enterprises making the shift to services at S_g start by building key relationships. These relationships are important because they broaden the purpose or vision of the enterprise by making a clear statement about the service that the enterprise wants to provide to society. In the food domain, these enterprises have formed partnerships with public institutions such as the American Heart Association, the National Cancer Institute, and the American Diabetes Association. Food enterprises proclaim these relationships proudly. For example, a few years ago, the news media reported on the findings of the National Cancer Institute that bran cereal aided in cancer prevention. Kellogg worked collaboratively with the National Cancer Institute and the Food and Drug Administration to raise our awareness of the beneficial effects of bran as Gus describes in Chapter 7.

At S_r, in addition to simply maintaining such relationships, food enterprises engage in joint research with public institutions to further our understanding of what good nutrition is and how it affects us. The results of this research help us learn what foods benefit us the most.

The official endorsement of, for example, a low-fat product makes us more certain about our personal food purchases. This is quite unlike the research done by the tobacco companies that they withheld from the public so that they could sell more cigarettes (that is, keep their product orientation) and jeopardize health. This example is a very striking differentiation between a product-oriented tobacco enterprise and a service enterprise in health and nutrition. In becoming a service, companies must change their behavior so that their impact on our health and environment becomes positive.

The food enterprises have been very effective at publishing the results of research in the S_s stage. A simple but highly effective example is the front of the Cheerios box that proudly proclaims its participation in an American Heart Association program and then uses the back of the cereal box to give us more information. The backs of most cereal boxes contain advertisements to sell gadgets and gimmicks to children who can collect enough box tops to make the purchase. What we are really saying is that cereal boxes are often valuable real estate used to sell more cereal. Giving up that advertising space to promote health and nutrition is a good example of an enterprise that is making the shift from a product mentality to a service mentality. It should also be a profitable shift. After all, buying a cereal because it is healthful for our children is a lot more rewarding than buying it to satisfy our children's desires for the trinkets the boxes sell.

Making the shift from products to services is an evolutionary step that any enterprise can make if it so chooses. That is not to say that it is an easy shift. It does require changing the underlying motivation of the company to see its role in causing beneficial community evolution. The next shift, from the third stage to the fourth, can be an even greater stretch.

CREATING IDEAL INTENTION

The fourth stage (the transformation stage) on the food domain map is our opportunity to use the METAMATRIX® to envision the future of the food domain. It is for that reason a hope and a prayer on our part. In the first three stages, we looked at activities of actual enterprises within the food domain to create our map entries. At T_g, we are for the most part looking to see the abundant and prosperous future we can create together in the food domain.

The transform (T) stage of the food domain map is a statement of the potential contribution that the food domain can ultimately make to humanity. It is a vision for what the food domain can become while it still exists in the information age on the map of human evolution. A more pragmatic way of describing this stage is that it sets a vision for where we can go. With that vision, we can start the journey to make it a reality.

The vision, or ideal intention, that we hold for the food domain is that it will work with nature to promote abundance for all life, that in its work, it benefits not only humanity but also our environment and our planet. We recognize that as a tall order, and we believe we can carry it out. Every enterprise would take a different approach to achieving the vision. We show one viable plan for achieving our vision in the fourth stage of the food domain map. It proceeds as follows.

A company that started by fully understanding its current impact on all life at T_g would be off to a good start. Having gathered that full understanding, the enterprise could then redesign as much of its processes, products, and services as needed to make them beneficial to all life. Service to life becomes the repeatable, *de facto* standard for the enterprise. With this beneficial base on which to build, the enterprise could then think about what it would take to end malnutrition worldwide in five years at the T_s stage. For example, one food company is doing research into what it would take to grow sufficiently hearty and productive indigenous grains worldwide to feed humanity. This company can foresee a future without hunger. Once we reach this plateau, achieving a vision that supports all life on earth is well within our reach. Once we create a vision for our domain that we truly believe in, that vision will stay with us. It will raise the ante for everything we do in meeting our daily goals and will inspire us to strive harder. It is the vision that pulls people together and motivates us to work for its success.

We look at a lot of ideas in this chapter and hold out a great deal of hope for both enterprises and humanity, and our collective ability to grow, mature ideally, and prosper. As we leave this chapter, we want to be sure that we leave you with the forests as well as the trees. In summary, we reiterate the themes of our first two ideal intentions:

- *Evolution is the only business.* All enterprises, both for-profit and nonprofit must create a vision for the future of their domain and their part in that future. Failure to do so risks extinction.
- *Life is the only customer.* The shift from products to services is more than a shift from proliferation to conscious evolution. It is a purposeful and thoughtful decision that widens and deepens opportunities for growth and profits in both the enterprise and the community. It is, in effect, the coevolution of the enterprise and humanity through the building of new, life-enhancing relationships.

Our map of human evolution provides a broad context for all human activity and thought, including domain mapping, which we have located at R_s on the larger map. The work of domain mapping, and all R_s work, is contemporary and grounded in reality. Humanity has evolved to R_s on the map.

As we conclude our discussion of domain mapping, we start looking to the future and to our opportunities to influence humanity's next evolutionary step. The task of envisioning and defining the future is a daunting one for everyone, including chief evolutionary officers. In the next chapter, Gus looks at some of the questions raised by the desire to create a new time of renaissance.

11

Creating Conscious Renaissance: R_t Time

In writing this chapter on the chief evolutionary officer (CEO) as cocreator and social architect of a conscious renaissance, we are starting to talk about the future. We are talking about repeating-transform (R_t), the eighth stage, the next stage, on the METAMATRIX® map of our species evolution. This stage of human evolution is just beginning to unfold within us and ahead of us. It is where we are going.

The carrying costs and the demands of increasing human population and our current scientific industrial culture on the environmental life of our planet, in combination with many other life-threatening pressures, signal the necessary transformation of human life on earth. What is in question is the nature of that planetary change and what we can do to bring about renaissance and evolution rather than devolution or collapse. What is already within us that is the seed long waiting to flower? What will unfold from within to lead us beyond life as our only customer to life's becoming our guide and mentor reborn anew, triumphant, and enduring?

TIME OF REBIRTH

The CEO has a leading role in helping the seed of evolutionary success unfold and express, from within the emerging human soul, our next guiding force of evolution. Our souls alone and together are waiting to serve us at this time of transformation of human cultural evolution. As DNA guides the unfolding of our biological being, so does a conscious, creative, collaborative, and compassionate soul guide our whole human species' spiritual unfolding, our strongest saving power.

How can we from the depth of our own souls as CEOs, begin to imagine and formulate the emerging stage of transformation of our fast-changing human species evolution? How can we create a conscious renaissance born of new values? How can we release some of the energy from the dynamic of replication and multiplication central to science, industry, and communication so that the next sharing dynamic can be built? In partial answer to these questions, in Part III of this book we look at the sharing dynamic that builds on the integration of differences. These dynamics use the synergetic union of differences. They focus on the primacy of relationships the purpose of which is the release of new potential for compassionate collaboration with natural order and all life on the planet.

On the METAMATRIX® map of human evolution, this time just emerging is R_t, the eighth of sixteen stages. R_t is the transformation of our civilization built on the repeat dynamic of replication of likeness and the repetition of principles, products, and practices so fundamental to our contemporary science-, industry-, and information-based lives. On our map, it is a turning point, the central balance point, the fulcrum of leverage for the continued health of our human evolution. In METAMATRIX® terms, we are entering the half-way-home moment of human evolutionary fulfillment. R_t truly is a renaissance time.

Never before has the whole human species had to undertake a redefinition of identity and formulate its ideal intention for the future in a conscious way. The magnitude of that challenge and responsibility dwarfs any and all great prior works of world import that humanity has accomplished. The physical, mental, emotional, and spiritual aspects of what it means to be human are all undergoing changes. That is the nature of times of transformation. Of all the growth stages, transformation is the least predictable because its dynamic calls for a totally new identity of higher order, a new grand synthesis of unity. The caterpillar becomes a butterfly. The human becomes a cosmic cocreator.

TIME OF QUESTIONING

There is another aspect of times of transformation. They are about "what if" questions, hypotheses, and imagined potentials. They are not so much times of realization and material manifestation as they are of conceptualization, ideation, and idealization. In that regard, it is a time for consideration of the best possible actions, values, and outcomes, a kind of a time-out from regular cultural time, a timeless time. Intuitive, imaginative, and visionary thinking is at a premium. It is a time for the highest spiritual ideas and ideals to reemerge for consideration. As I have said before, idealism is the mother of practicality. The highest ideals are always the most elegantly simple and powerful, practical, and archetypal forms and processes whether they are seeds for mighty trees or sacraments for mighty truths.

For the CEO this is a profound time of personal change. The CEO is asked for a new, soul-felt code of values, a new meaning in life, and a new image of creative enterprise and social organization. Now that we assert that the business of all our business is evolution, how do we proceed? What values, images, and ideals will bring our intentions and actions into balance and harmony with the long-term life enhancement and soul fulfillment of human and planetary evolution?

In the several-million-year history of human evolution and with the recent incredible acceleration of change now becoming visible, the next decades of transformation are but a moment. They are decades of time out of time to rediscover and rebirth humanity. Like the frescoes on the Sistine Chapel ceiling by Michelangelo, the whole painting of what humanity can be is a new painting. That picture is totally ours to make as a species consciously and collaboratively. It is the artwork of the CEOs and their colleagues, all humanity.

The empty painting surface is the sky, sea, and land of the earth. As vanishing-point perspective was born in the first renaissance, evolving-point perspective is emerging in our renaissance, so well symbolized by the image of earth from space. We have evolved amazing abilities in our physical and mental reality with the cosmology introduced by Einstein in which the upper limit of reality is light and electricity that we can see and feel with our bodies. Now, however, we are called beyond light speed in our human evolutionary unfolding. We are called to evoke and discover the superluminal realms of our being inside us waiting to emerge and guide us. We are evolving into creative endeavor in the timeless human realm of soul and spirit.

Beyond light and electricity, all of us are being asked, what is the business of the human soul and spirit and the deeper self within? What are the values, the dynamics, the new coin of that realm of evolution?

A TIME FOR SOCIAL ARCHITECTURE

In asking how to approach the realm of conscious evolution at this juncture, it is time to offer aspiring CEOs another useful perspective, mentioned earlier but not yet defined. All conscious evolutionaries and especially CEOs are inventors and creators of our future society; they are social architects. That name has been used by historians and social commentators to speak of the work of people like Thomas Jefferson who have worked to create new and greater social well-being.

Starting in Florence in 1978 and in a focused way in the last decade, I have been working to synthesize emerging social needs and concepts of natural order. The idea has been to make social architecture into a new, active form of art, science, and design. In this way, social architecture can be a service to help the evolution of all our businesses become the new business of evolution. I believe that social architecture is a way to meet our need to create the best possible conscious social evolution.

For example, in a project with a group of leading designers of organizational learning at Chase Manhattan Bank, I created a METAMATRIX®-based learning assessment and design instrument. The group defined its own terms for natural and necessary developmental stages of the four aspects of physical, mental, relational, and intentional learning. We were able to identify learning needs for employees and consider the design process of that learning. We were working toward a harmonious balancing and synthesis of the four chosen aspects of learning. This instrument was later developed into a generic learning guide called the Human Fulfillment Factor™.

Along the way, I felt called to begin to synthesize the ancient arts of sacred architecture with the emerging ideal of social architecture. In seeking to advance this new form of design creativity, to evolve it, I went to Monticello, Thomas Jefferson's beautiful home estate. There I prayed for help in defining social architecture. Early on Easter morning of that visit, I wrote the following: "Social Architecture is divine grace revealed in natural order used for the planning and enhancement of human fulfillment." That definition has proved to be so profound and succinct that I have felt resistance to changing it.

Grace and wisdom are natural gifts from beneficent life and life's conscious harmonious orderliness. They are the divinely intended loving gifts of generosity from the universe. That generosity is revealed in all the amazingly elegant structures and processes of natural order— geese in migration, galaxies in spin, spiders in webs.

If we can use that grace-filled natural order for human planning and enhancement of all life on the planet, we are becoming social architects. Becoming wise users of natural order is why we have emphasized our discovery of a pattern of general periodicity and made it a thinking and design tool for you in the METAMATRIX® and its domain-mapping applications. These design tools are for you as social architects and for your planning and enhancement of human fulfillment. We suggest that part of contemporary human ful- fillment is an all-win-for-planetary-life transformation of our values and behavior dependent in large measure on our spiritual unfolding and maturation. The power and wisdom for healthy human and planetary conscious evolution lie within us. In uniting our souls in reverence and creativity, we advance the order, life, and love of the universe.

The work of social architecture can be the work of the soul for CEOs. The subject of soul is becoming a central concern and focus of our culture. There are more than 200 recently published books on the subject of soul and more than 2,000 with the word soul in the title. If we simply say that soul is the vessel in us, that essence of our being that relates us and binds us to our spiritual purpose for living, then social architecture can be soul work.

Our souls can hear the call from the divine grace and wisdom of the universe. Our souls can connect us with the divine intention revealed in natural order. They can enhance the fulfilling of our lives with our conscious evolution of love.

My futurist mentors have offered me inspiring ideas that make them social architects as well as visionary CEOs. Buckminster Fuller spoke of love as the steel of the next millennium. Margaret Mead spoke of reorienting our intention in science to resonance with and reverence for the subjects of our consideration—a resanctification of how we learn and know. Barbara Hubbard has created and hosted social inven- tions to enable the experience of cocreation of conscious evolution. These social architects have offered us great leadership in designing evolutionary initiatives.

One of the principles that social architect Bucky Fuller offers as grace and wisdom is what he calls the natural order of "ephemeralization," the conscious human ability to do more and more with less and less. One of Fuller's favorite examples was that by adding other metals to iron, transformatively uniting and synthesizing differences into a higher unity, we can create steel light enough for the skin of an airplane wing. A second favorite was that by replacing tons of transoceanic cable with lightweight communication satellites, we can continuously ephemeralize our creative place in nature.

Doing more with less is a conscious human evolutionary value, principle, and practice worthy of becoming part of the architecture of our evolutionary endeavors. Fuller did this especially well in his social invention and architecture of the Dymaxion World Map and World Game that help us find how to integrate and ephemeralize all our human behavior and natural resources into one planetary evolutionary success story. Fuller's World Game is a model for our own evolutionary experimentation now under way.

Margaret Mead gave us grace and wisdom for conscious evolutionary design in her ideal value, principle, and practice of seeking organic natural models and designs for our social inventions and scientific searching. For example, Mead's call is being answered in the contemporary field of biomimicry, in which we use the ancient wisdom found deep in life forms and ecological systems. From that wisdom, biomimicry helps to develop ideas and methods for acting in reverent harmony with life and doing more with less guided by the natural order graced to us by countless life forms.

The spider is one such teacher. One spider filament is hundreds of times stronger and more flexible than its equivalent weight and size in steel filament. Mead asks us how we can learn more of nature's power and ideal ephemeralization for the design of our own communities.

Margaret Mead helped to formulate the two new sciences of general systems theory and cybernetics. These fields of study aid us in finding an architectural process that underlies our efforts at conscious creative evolution. By focusing us on resonance and reverence, Mead is asking us to create our own new forms of science to meet our evolving needs as social architects.

Barbara Hubbard is a leading visionary advocate and social architect of conscious evolution, exemplified in her book, *Conscious Evolution: Awakening the Power of Our Social Potential* (1998). Barbara has been enacting the principles of transformation by gathering, repeating, and sharing ideas, contexts, events, and relationships to seek and find a higher order unity of human and social potential. She calls the time we are living in the birth of universal humanity, a time when we are learning ethical evolution, reverent protection, and regeneration of life on earth. From her initiatives of political leadership, to citizen diplomacy, to SYNCON meetings for inner city gang leaders in Los Angeles, Barbara's work has exemplified the social architecture of conscious evolution.

My own decision to establish social architecture as a new form of art, science, and design and my practice of it evolved through several stages. Hosting Bucky Fuller's World Game at Boston College in 1970 and participating in several SYNCONs in the early 1970s helped transform my own work as an artist from painting and film making to experimental video productions and large group process events documented and exhibited as conceptual art works in Boston.

After presenting two works at the Boston Museum of Fine Arts as part of a show at the museum school, I began to question the egoic politics of the art world. One of my video works in the museum taped a panel of artists speaking on the limits of conceptual art. Some of these artists participated in the work, called *Delayed Acceleration,* for the year of its duration. I videotaped them and played the tape back to them, folding each tape of watching and listening into the next. The series of taped events progressed from the first second that the artists began to speak, to the next minute, to the next hour, to reconvening at intervals of a day, week, month, and year of their self-study.

The process of self-scrutiny, at first fun, became ultimately nauseating for all of us. It drove me out of the art world for good, and I began to design events purely for the common good of the participants and society. In 1974, I staged a three-day conference on the future of television at the experimental studio of WGBH, the PBS station in Boston. Using builder's staging, we built a three-story diamond-cubic setting with 12 opposing platforms for 12 separate conversations on the future. The diamond crystal-shaped set for the conference was based on Derald Langham's Genesa models. Derald participated in the event as a most valuable wise elder.

During the three days everyone got to go to each platform to discuss each of the 12 perspectives on the future and share their ideas with the other 11 groups. The surprising success of this event set the stage for the "Town Meeting 2000" in which Barbara Hubbard and I teamed with our two crews to broadcast the future aspect of the opening of the United States Bicentennial Celebration in April of 1975.

On my first of three trips to England and Italy in 1977 to work on staging the First World Congress of the New Age, I filled out the occupation space on the landing card for Heathrow Airport with the title "social architect," self-named for the first time. That congress was an experiment in the social architecture of an unstructured open agenda for ten days running. After the repeated trials and shocks of necessarily continuous social inventions and collaboration, in closing we achieved a transformation: a spontaneous act of whole-group worship without a word spoken. We moved and sang in celebration for an hour of pure joy.

After the Florence event, I designed and videotaped an event for a regional initiative called *Forum on the Valley Future* involving representatives from 52 Vermont and New Hampshire towns of the upper valley of the Connecticut River. Participants generated plans and priorities for future collaborative social inventions to help evolve their region. My edited videotape of the event helped win a three-year grant from the National Science Foundation to continue the forum process and establish many of the planners' dreams.

During the 1980s, most of my work to establish social architecture and use the METAMATRIX® for evolutionary thinking was done in the corporate and education sectors. In Europe, I worked with British Petroleum in London, Credit Suisse in Zurich, and IMD in Lausanne; in Canada, Toronto Dominion Bank and Northern Telecom; and in the United States, Arthur Andersen, The American Society of Training and Development, AT&T, Chase Manhattan Bank, JC Penney, Micromentor, P.W. Minor, Pillsbury, Polaroid, and Xerox. I also had the good fortune to work at the Massachusetts Institute of Technology and with Michael Ray at the Stanford Business School to bring some METAMATRIX® thinking to graduate students and professionals.

In this decade, I have continued that kind of corporate and non-profit work while helping to introduce and advance the ideas and practice of social architecture at the Creative Problem Solving Institute and elsewhere. While starting the researching, creating, and writing of a cosmology of love, I have worked collaboratively with a small learning community in Vermont to enact and teach the C4 values (consciousness, creativity, collaboration, compassion) we offer and aspire to in this book.

From these two decades of work, I have come to believe that social architecture is a mode of endeavor that serves the creation of social and environmental well-being and healthy evolution. As we go forward to consider its use, we will be finding many ways to champion all our ideal intentions on evolution, life, community, and love. In Part III, we use the definition and practice of social architecture as an example of the kind of creative action needed from CEOs as we formulate the new sharing stage of conscious human evolution.

Part III

Community Is the Only Profit

This is the second time in the history of our species that we have come to realize that the quality of our soul service and life fulfillment gets its measure directly from the quality of our life in community. The first time was in the long, ancient traditions of indigenous culture wherein value given to community was value in life. Meaning and value in life come from what we bring and give to community in free and willing association with all life. In this way, we are now beginning to understand that collaborative, compassionate communities of all kinds and sizes form the vessel and the architecture of our evolution. They also become the fulcrums for the leverage we need to cocreate a healthy future with all life on earth. We therefore seek to help you create from the reality that community is the only profit.

12

Community: Evolution's Vessel

As we journey together into the unknown sharing and transforming stages of future human evolution, our ideas and visions are offered as design elements and suggestions for chief evolutionary officers (CEOs) acting as social architects. We realize that both these roles are works in progress. We are seeking and learning how to consciously become humans newly awakened to a higher potential beneficence to all our relations. In this chapter we offer perspectives on why we focus on building new communities of intentional meaning and purpose, how a definition of evolution is itself evolving, where we find our place in the web of life, and how human values in community life are themselves a new form of profit.

This book, in four parts, follows the sequence of gathering, repeating, sharing, and transforming in its presentation of the four insights, each of which is the title of a part. Part III is the sharing stage of our book. In the sharing stage of the METAMATRIX®, we focus on the integration of differences. That coming-together process is fitting for the subject of communities and how they profit their members.

We gather our book with the ideal intention that evolution is the only business. Evolution is also the biggest gathering process we know. Life also is the necessary repeating and repeatable carrier of the evolutionary success process and pattern. Life is ultimately the only customer because it is the prime carrier of the evolutionary process and of a sustainable future. To survive and flourish, the evolution of human culture must sustain the evolution of all life.

Our ideal intention is that community becomes the vessel in which healthy evolution in support of life occurs. As nature provides the context for the integration and interaction of all life, community provides the context for human integration and organization. In that sense, community can become the enabler of almost everything that is desirable for successful conscious planetary evolution. On the continuum between individuals and the planet, we have decided to place the fulcrum at communities.

Community is another name for the multiple relationships that make life work. In any domain or area of enterprise, the quality of creative community determines the quality of productivity, profitability, and sustainability. This need for effective community is as important within nonprofit enterprises, such as cities and towns and Internet groups, as it is within for-profit enterprises that emphasize internal teamwork and strong external relationships with suppliers and customers.

Community culture is the new focus of concern that is the host generator of profitability. Any form of negative destruction of community from crime to terrorist behavior is an obvious example of the destruction of the creative process and mutual profitability. Conversely, in the knowledge era, profit is collaborative learning and synergistic creation that brings about increased financial, social, and environmental well-being.

The phrase *financial, social, and environmental well-being* implies a relation among those three; you cannot have one without the others. In Parts I and II we talk about healthy evolution supporting life as the only real and important customer. Now we say that community also is the means of creating life-serving relationships that result in financial, environmental, and community profit, or social well-being.

COMMUNITY REDEFINED

Community in this moment in human evolution needs to be redefined as an ideal, a goal, a joint project consciously entered into by all its members, all life. A recent example of the need for rethinking and redesign presents itself in the emerging challenge of designing space communities for large numbers of people in orbit around the earth.

This design challenge for how to export, sustain, and regenerate life where none has been before helps us to focus on our own planetary communities aboard what Buckminster Fuller called "Spaceship Earth."

We need to augment our thinking of space colonies beyond technological considerations and start thinking about the individual, social, and environmental needs for living, not mere subsistence, in space. The space challenge can become the second term in a metaphor of earth space helping us learn more about how to heal, regenerate, and coevolve life on earth. It is one of many design challenges that help us learn a way to revive the sacred balances and harmonies inherent in the natural order of all life. In this way, life will prevail, and the awakening and fulfillment of the soul story of humanity will be one of nurturing life on earth and in space.

In our definition of community, we can take our guiding ideal intentions of evolution, life, community, and love and use them as part of the process of redefining community. We might consider the ideal that evolution can be continuous creation. Life can be inter- and intraspecies creative collaboration. Community can be the context for compassion that allows us to foster creative collaboration with all past, present, and future life. And love can be an experience of communion felt in conscious, creative, collaborative, compassionate (C4) community.

WEB OF LIFE

This is the second time in history that humanity may be coming into awareness of the primacy of community. Traditional indigenous cultures always had, and now have, all things as their relations in equal respect and gratitude. They consider humans to be brothers and sisters to all creation in a mutually supportive family that we call nature. That interrelatedness with each other within nature and that mutual support are part of our definition of community. The call to community now has to do with reuniting ourselves with nature and each other. It has to do with reawakening to our place in the web of life—the web of universal love—in a gracious, humble, and grateful way.

In earth's environment, we are rapidly approaching an all-win or all-lose situation with respect to the viability of all species, humankind

included. Contemporary writing about ecological issues lately indicates that we are heading toward a dire situation. In his book *The Ecology of Commerce*, Paul Hawken (1993) cites the fact that human beings are now claiming 40 percent of the earth's production, by both direct and indirect means, for ourselves. In *The Diversity of Life*, Edward O. Wilson (1992) details his conclusion that we are now in one of the great eras of extinction of entire species in our planet's history. Janine Benyus (1997) in her book *Biomimicry* states that pesticides and nitrates from fertilizer are having a deadly effect on rural agricultural families by leaching into ground water. Looking at these three situations together, we can gain a strong sense of the jeopardy in which we currently place ourselves and all life on our planet.

Holistic all-win well-being is the evermore apparent necessity for sustainable planetary life. Sustainable and regenerative life and love are ideal outcomes of human fulfillment. They are the true ultimate profit. Community is the central dynamic context and most viable focus and domain of action to achieve this profit in size, complexity, and workable relationships for all-win life. Compassionate community and its quality of holistic well-being are the source, the way, and the measure of full life profit. That is a summation of what we mean when we reach for the ideal intention that community is the only profit.

EVOLVING EVOLUTION

Finding our place in the web of life is a critical aspect of defining symbiotic relationships within the web of life. How we locate our place in that web has fascinating implications for how we see the world around us. Seeing ourselves as part of the natural evolutionary process is quite different from seeing nature as separate from us, as an object to be studied and controlled. Talking about evolution in terms of finding our place in the web of life also is quite different from studying the evolution of an individual species.

A prime implication of the concept of the web of life is the idea that evolution also has moved beyond the Darwinian notion of competitive survival of the fittest to the notions of symbiosis, integration, and synergy. The pressing awareness is that the whole of our natural planetary ecology has to succeed or none of it will succeed. It is a time for learning to be synergists who can help learn from nature and find a way to protect and enhance life and guarantee its regeneration. These synergists are CEOs.

It is no longer a question of survival of the parts but survival of the whole. We are coming to realize that as the dominant and domineering life form on the planet, we have responsibility for the long-term viability of life. In this context, the place where creative action and healthy life is the most physical, visible, and measurable is in the relationships of our communities, for example, local neighborhoods, work groups, or groups connected over the Internet.

We see the current movement toward sustainable communities as an example of the link between a healthy earth, human health, and healthy communities. The notion of sustainability, as it is being defined in numerous communities across this country, is an acknowledgment of our interdependence as humans and our interdependence with the success of all life on our planet. Therefore we can say that healthy community is the fulcrum of future human evolution. It is the sphere of creative action of which we all are a part and that we can most readily influence with our good intentions and values.

BEYOND DARWINISM

If, as Darwin did, we look at the evolution of single species, it is understandable that competition would emerge as a critical value. However, the minute we focus the concept of evolution on the ecology of the whole planet, the interdependence and integration of all species together become the paramount subject and dynamic of our redefinition of evolution. Concepts such as synergy and symbiosis become important new dynamics of ecological evolution. Survival of the fittest as the sole focus becomes inappropriate and eventually hostile to the well-being of the whole of life and the planet.

In the light of the redefinition of evolution from that of a species to that of all life, purposeful or intentional community is an enactment of ideal evolutionary activity made so by conscious, creative, collaborative compassion. Single-species orientation, or single-enterprise orientation, is dysfunctional in a planetary ecological and economic context. Competition has to be placed in the context of collaboration, cooperation, and alliance—conscious membership in the planetary ecological success story. Human consciousness and the marketplace are fast requiring of all participants that they become conscious, creative, collaborative, and compassionate for life on earth.

The fragile state of our environment necessitates treating it as a whole. All of us may not have the same level of exposure to the idea that treating the worldwide economy as a whole also makes sense. To elaborate, we are beginning to sense that the world environment and the world economy are one and the same. Indigenous peoples and farming cultures have always known this. If we shift our focus from economic to bionomic, to the notion that all life is the community of exchange, then the world economy becomes the world bionomy. And, as we have said, all life itself is always the first and last customer in line to acquire our goods and services and report on whether we are exploitive or regenerative. The bionomy of life has to transform the marketplace into the whole planetary environmental setting for our activities of commerce. The shift is from financial gain to ecological well-being.

C4 community is emerging as the real profit driving all other activity toward its fulfillment. The environmental movement is joined by the social responsibility movement, the sustainability movement, and even the awakening to voluntary simplicity. As these values continue to integrate and evolve in their mutual power, healthy community—C4 community—becomes evermore obvious as the profit of all current enterprise. Any bold visible initiatives in this emerging value system will win and are winning the profitable approval of the world marketplace, and the economy becomes the bionomy.

An excellent example of this is the Findhorn community in the north of Scotland, where I gave a talk at a conference in 1977. Since its spiritual inception and its miraculous stories of growth of plants in concert with the spirits of nature, Findhorn has inspired and educated a whole generation of social inventors and social entrepreneurs. Their communities and contributions and businesses have shown extraordinary earth-healing profitability both financially and spiritually. Findhorn is really a graduate school of emerging global goodness, conscious evolution, and collaborative alliances.

Collaborative alliances that make a profitable union from differences and different gifts are the new winning strategy for all enterprises in the contemporary global culture. We've learned the importance of collaboration and cooperation in everything from the disarming of nuclear weapons to the care of the world's fisheries and forests. Conservation and a host of other challenges are, of necessity, topics and initiatives that require multinational cooperation and collaboration. As we clearly see with Chernobyl and the Amazon rain forests, local stress, accident, and depletion are a planetary concern. As those engaged in recycling know, we cannot throw things away; there is no more away.

The challenge before all of humanity right now is that of balancing and harmonizing earth's generativity, our well-being, and the use of our common wealth. The challenge of creating communities that redefine prosperity and profit in a way that supports all life is a tremendous need in the work of creating conscious evolution. It is a time to reach for the ideal intention that community is the only profit.

FUTURE HUMAN EVOLUTION

Community is the fulcrum of human evolution. All the evolutionary initiatives by individuals, families, and groups can have tremendous influence on the evolution of the larger social organization of states, nations, the human species as a whole, and the planet. The reverse also is true: the large groups can help evolve the small groups and individuals. Yet none of it can happen without passing through and pivoting on community. As community goes, so goes human evolution.

That is, undoubtedly, a strong assertion, especially in the face of so many contemporary forces that are so obviously destroying things that in the past have given us a feeling of home and belonging in city neighborhood or town or village. We need to rethink and reinvent community so that a new form of ideal relations can be created to fulfill the soul journeys of all its members as they reunite in an everdeepening compassion for the whole web of life.

A pioneer C4 community is a gathering of active thinkers who have decided to take full responsibility for creating their context, their relationships, and their behavior toward evolving their higher individual and social potential in an intentional community. As social architects, CEOs may find these three responsibilities important in reverse order: intention and behavior first, relationships next, and context or location last.

I lived for a time in an intentional community of Sufis called The Abode in New Lebanon, New York. The community was situated on 450 acres of land and used and rejuvenated the abandoned buildings of part of the original central community of Shakers. The confluence of those two spiritual traditions in that place gave it tremendous power of potential. The combination of the Shaker saying "Hands to work, and hearts to God" and the Universal Worship service of the Sufis' honoring all the world's religions made for the intentions, relations, and context of a truly pioneering C4 community.

The Abode, a community of 50 adults and 20 children, achieved a remarkable degree of food and wood-fuel self-sufficiency. We ran our own elementary school, a retreat and conference center, a year-long calendar of cultural, musical, and learning events, a regular Sunday worship service, daily mediation services, and the education for ordination of our spiritual leaders. An extended family beyond The Abode used this community as the touchstone of their ideals and beliefs. This extended family came from all over the world.

Like the Findhorn family, The Abode family, while seeking to ground their idealism in working and living together and while opening their hearts to the fulfillment of soul and spirit together, are creating an extended family of pioneers in human personal and social evolution through their own kind of C4 community. In the oftenexhausting physical, emotional, and spiritual struggles and amid times of great joy and holiness, the overriding focus and well-earned sense of pride is not personal but communal.

These kinds of intentional communities can form around initiatives in business, education, medicine, or any domain of human endeavor. It is my belief, however, that if they do not have a spiritual intention at their center held jointly by their members, these communities are in danger of spinning apart rather than together. In the formation of a community, it can well be said that gather, repeat, share, transform (GRST) also works in reverse. The T, power of spiritual intent, grows the S, the sharing of synergetic relationships uniting many differences, which grows the R ᵗhe repetition of all the daily necessities and activities, which gr⎯⎯⎯⎯ ⏌ e G, the gathering of a pioneer C4 community.

Community is our ideal intention. The design and hosting of community are a focus for CEOs as social architects. We focus our next stage of human evolution on all-life relations and the creation of pioneer C4 community in our developing map of human evolution (Figure 12–1).

		Independent Nations	Collaborative Alliances	All-life Relations	Universal Love
	Transform	Dark ages	Create conscious renaissance	Transform values into peace and health in all relations	**Tt**
	Share	City states	Information age	Share global C4 value news	**Ts**
	Repeat	Agriculture	Industrial age	Create C4 communities and values in all contexts	**Tr**
G R O W T H	**Gather**	Hunter/ gatherer	Renaissance: science and reason	Pioneer C4 communities and values	**Tg**

TIME ⟶

Figure 12–1 *Sharing Stage of Human Evolution*

PIONEERING C4 COMMUNITIES (S$_G$)

People enjoy scanning the future of many captivating subjects, such as science, technology, the economy, and politics. We have chosen to synthesize an all-inclusive context for these and all other subjects with our evolutionary focus on the subject of pioneer C4 communities. We feel that C4 evolutionary values and communities are the seeds and the settings for the giant future trees of the human soul and spirit.

The greatest financial success in human affairs springs from the creation of the archetypal products of an age. In the early industrial age, it was the steel of Andrew Carnegie, the oil of John D. Rockefeller, the automobiles of Henry Ford. Now in our age of information and knowledge, the archetypal product of software is pushing Bill Gates of Microsoft toward the possibility of being the world's first trillionaire. Yet we see the story of human evolution now poised to transform the ideals and the concepts of human value.

We suggest that the values are evolving from steel to software to soul to spirit. We suggest that the evolution from human physical production to mental creation to spiritual fulfillment is built into our personal and species development so deeply and so undeniably that its emergence is inevitable and unstoppable. Therefore, an investment in the social architecture of any form of C4 community is a great and wise gift of soul energy, of love, to the story of human and earth evolution. It is the first step in the macrostage of sharing-gather, of human evolution at S$_g$ on the map.

COMMUNITY CONTEXTS (S$_R$)

For our second stage of the repeating of sharing, we envision the creating of C4 communities and values in all contexts. *All contexts* means that what we now sometimes experience in an inspiring church service, in visiting a monastery, or in standing in awe of a glorious sunset, that kind of full human experience, can be consciously created everywhere in homes, schools, workplaces, and in all our relations.

"All our relations" is a statement made by the Sioux and other Native Americans when they enter the holiness of their sweat lodge to pray and to tell the deepest truths of their souls and to see in total darkness what visions the Great Spirit may have for them. "All our relations" is a prayer of gratitude for all beings in the universe, from the stones of the fire to the birds of the air and all else we can ever know. Such a prayer in such a C4 ceremony as a sweat lodge in honor of all our relations is an example of what we mean by *all contexts*. That ceremony is a perfect example of sacred social architecture. It is a creative, collaborative, compassionate community of souls engaged in their full humanity, painfully, sorrowfully, and joyfully sweating out their deepest cares and truths together. Together they are cleansing, healing, and inspiring their personal and communal future.

GLOBAL C4 VALUE NEWS (S_S)

The next challenge to the CEO and sacred social architect is how to design and host a global sharing (S_s) of the C4 value news of ever deeper human fulfillment. What follows is an example of a scenario that may spark your imagination for your own design work.

Imagine a live television program shown everywhere in the world twenty-four hours a day called "DAWN." Imagine that at dawn in each successive time zone, alternating southern and northern hemisphere, we see the sun rise on some C4 initiatives in a C4 community within that time zone. The program features the youth of that place telling the world in their creative way their soul work and play for conscious evolution. Those watching can contribute their C4 news and available resources to each and every "DAWN" site that needs their help as they choose. The story is one of a world weaving its evolutionary fulfillment.

PEACE AND HEALTH IN ALL RELATIONS (S_T)

Imagine further that the transformation of the macrosharing stage of human evolution has found that the C4 values have transformed the world into a more peaceful and healthy place in all its relations. The emphasis of soul-centered learning, the guidance from the wisdom of the universe, and the intuitive mutual C4 bonding in community have played a role in the conscious fulfillment of all human soul stories and lives. This natural spiritual and behavioral evolution of all humans has brought with it a withering away of war, terrorism, and violence.

When it becomes clear that all these evils are based on fear and that fear is born of the absence of love, the whole interpersonal and political economic exchange dynamics transforms to include the currency of unconditional love.

These four stages of the macrosharing era in the map of human evolution are focused on community to help us create a context in which all our best evolutionary ideal values and intentions can and must play out. They ask us to imagine ideal outcomes of evolved human behavior. In a map of human learning in Chapter 14, I explain why I think these outcomes are built into our human nature and are ready to become manifest. When they do, our ideal intention that community is the only profit will be self-fulfilling.

13

Exploring C4 Community

Communities are our focus here and our ideal for the future. Communities can be rural towns or city neighborhoods. They can be based on heritage or other ethnic, cultural, and social bonds. They can be physical communities at a geographic site or virtual communities that share information using a variety of means, including the telephone and the Internet. Individual enterprises can be communities, and we are all familiar with the phrase "the business community."

In all cases, communities are groups of people who have relationships based on common interests. Gus refers to community as the fulcrum of human evolution. In saying that, he is indicating our hope that communal relationships are the key to future learning and evolution. Enriching those current relationships and extending them to an ever larger community of life is the potential that we see in the creation of conscious, creative, collaborative, and compassionate (C4) community.

Community is the focus of this part of our book because it is a vital way of acting out our role in the web of life. Community forms a clear and practical connection of high ideals and business realities. No matter how large or small a circle an enterprise draws to encompass its community, the reciprocal relationships and opportunities for mutual benefit are always before us. Community and enterprise are an ideal integration of human potential and practicality. I would like to share with you some stories that indicate to me the real possibility of creating C4 communities.

STORIES OF C4 COMMUNITIES

In thinking about the creation of C4 communities, most of us new to our role as chief evolutionary officer (CEO) likely feel that we are entering uncharted territory and taking risks in so doing. It is a realistic feeling. To help formulate an idea of what the future might look like, I am offering a few stories of events that have already taken place and that express movement toward the values of C4 community. These stories contain elements of conscious evolution, creativity, collaboration, and compassion and are significant because they describe actual situations, not future scenarios. None of these stories is an embodiment of our ideal intention of community as the only profit. Each does, however, provide a glimpse into future possibilities and potential. Each is a pioneer on the path to C4 community.

SALVAGING BLUEBEARD'S SHIP

National Public Radio's "Morning Edition" gave a wonderful account of a creative, collaborative project among for-profit and nonprofit enterprises that resulted in mutual benefit. In this case, the enterprises were a company, a university, a state government, and a community. The company, whose business is to find sunken treasure, located the ship of the infamous pirate Bluebeard. The ship was in 20 feet of water off the coast of the Carolinas. Usually when such a find occurs, the salvage company sells each recovered artifact to the highest bidder, thereby disassembling and dispersing the whole. This company, however, took a highly innovative approach to allocating the rights to the wreck.

The company is keeping only the book and movie rights to the wreck and is giving the actual ship, at its ocean site, to a university for archeological exploration. The understanding between the company and the university is that the university will bring the wreck to the surface and learn about the ship's history in the process. Working with the state, the university will give the entire contents of the wreckage site to a local community for assembly and public display. With the display, the community can share an interesting era of history and can generate revenue. Other communities are thinking of creating a Bluebeard theme park to draw tourists. The project is a verifiable case in which creative collaboration is resulting in community profit and financial profit for all involved.

COMMUNITY HEALTH INSURANCE

This story about community health insurance is one that Gus heard in his work with the health care industry. It is a good example of the care and compassion that communities can create for their members. With all the attention our health care system receives in the news media these days, this community's solution has always struck me as a creative one.

One of the visionary leaders in the redefinition of health returned from her work in Washington in the 1990s to her home town in the midwest. There she helped her community to become a health cooperative, self-insured and mutually caring and care giving. The community set up its own clinic that was sufficient for all but the most complicated and dire medical needs.

By setting up its own system of insurance and a clinic, the community retained all the money that community members would otherwise have spent in the world of health care and insurance. Keeping that money in town and investing it in their own cooperative gave the community the resources to improve the health of the population and to save enough money immediately to hire much-needed new teachers in the local school system.

This C4 community activity is so much healthier and more profitable than the nonintegrated and disconnected expenditure of everyone for his- or herself into the larger health care system. The community provides a context in which understanding and compassion find expression. This caring is in stark contrast to the competitive, survival-of-the-fittest philosophy of large, independent health insurers.

NUCOR STEEL

Nucor Steel is one of the few steel companies in the United States that have flourished in the 1990s. The company is successful because Nucor products are competitive in price and quality in the world markets. That success results from a management philosophy that puts a priority on the company's technology and its people. Nucor's relationship with its employees is of particular interest to us as an example of collaborative community within an enterprise and of an enterprise's relationship with the larger community in which it resides.

Nucor is known for its commitment to its workforce. The company proudly points to the fact that "during the past 20 years, Nucor has not laid off a single worker due to lack of work. The result is a committed team of Nucor employees that looks ahead to a bright future" (www.nucor.com/story.htm). Nucor does more, however, than simply provide job security. The Nucor Web page highlights the following ways in which all workers are part of the Nucor community:

- Employees, except for company officers, benefit from a profit-sharing plan derived from a minimum of 10% of pretax earnings.
- Nucor describes itself as having a flat and decentralized management structure and egalitarian policies that emphasize teamwork and open lines of communication between workers and management.
- Nucor chooses sites in nonurban locations where it feels it can establish strong relationships with both its workforce and the larger community.

Nucor's commitment to its employees has created a workforce the company describes as hardworking and dedicated. That workforce repays the company for its commitment.

CLEARING OVERGROWTH WITH SHEEP

To maintain ready access to power lines in New Hampshire's rough terrain, Public Service Company of New Hampshire (PSNH) has to clear away vegetation in the paths of the power lines (*The Valley News*, Saturday, April 25, 1998). In the past, the company has done this with work crews and by spraying herbicides. As an experiment this summer, PSNH is contracting for sheep to do this work.

The use of sheep is nothing new. Before machinery took over the job, use of sheep to clear land was common. PSNH's hope is that the sheep will prove to be more cost effective than work crews with machinery and herbicides and that neighbors will see these herbivorous animals as an improvement over unwanted herbicides.

LAND INSTITUTE IN KANSAS

As we focus more on the larger world community and on our interdependence with all life, we need to invent new kinds of relationships beyond human ones. An example of the level of caring and compassion for the earth itself is communities that focus their creativity on the emerging activity of permaculture and biomimicry in agriculture. Both of these activities entail learning from nature to transform agriculture from exploitive and petroleum-dependent practices to sustainable and regenerative patterns. Perennial plants are used in combination with appropriate new harvesting processes. These communities of pioneers are using nature's ways to reinvent agriculture.

A primary example is the Land Institute in Kansas. This group is rejuvenating a small prairie community while reengaging the wisdom of the prairie ecology as a guide to the future of farming. This institute is working to revolutionize farming by moving beyond dependence on fertilizers and pesticides to using nature's successful farming practices. A Web page for the Land Institute and its director Wes Jackson states that the institute is "guided by the ideal that the most rational agriculture for any region is the one based on the least elusive standard for sustainability: nature" (www.seedballs.com.agrpa.html).

Modern agriculture currently plants monocultures, for example, a wheat field or a corn field, whereas nature plants in polycultures, for example, a prairie with a great diversity of grasses and other plants and animals. Monocultures require tilling and fertilizers, which cause soil erosion and pollution. Polycultures are self-sustaining and environmentally friendly.

The work of the Land Institute is an investment in the future that is extremely important. A growing number of farmers use organic agriculture, but the concept of learning from and mimicking nature's ways to create sustainable agriculture is innovative and refreshing. This learning from nature extends our feeling of community beyond our cities, towns, work groups, and Internet colleagues to the land itself. That connection with and reverence for land, that is, for earth itself, has been an important human value for most of our evolutionary history. Now we have the opportunity to figure out how that connection and reverence plays out in our time.

CREATING C4 COMMUNITY

As we examine the role of CEOs in creating C4 communities, we can offer design concepts and tools of social architecture that will help CEOs envision and build a creative and collaborative future. The design concepts center on the dynamics of the sharing stage of the METAMATRIX®. These are the philosophical framework for this creative C4 work. The design tools are a tightly interrelated set of METAMATRIX® maps. They start with the map of human evolution and lend understanding to the process of creating C4 community. Particular emphasis is placed on the learning needed for everyone to commit to and share C4 values.

DYNAMICS OF SHARING

Using the dynamics of the METAMATRIX® share stage provides CEOs with a way of thinking that encourages the conceptualization and design of C4 communities. We talk about the share stage as being the integration of differences. By sandwiching the concept of integration between symbiosis and synergy, we describe the process-pattern of METAMATRIX® sharing.

Symbiosis

The term *symbiosis* is used most commonly in science to describe a mutually beneficial relationship between two entities. Perhaps the most profound and all-encompassing example of symbiosis is the relationship that oxygen-breathing animal species have with plant species. We depend on plants for the oxygen they produce, and plants depend on animal life for the carbon dioxide we exhale. Our very breath supports plant life, and plants support us.

Interestingly enough, this symbiotic relationship between plants and animals is an example of nature's efficiency. In nature nothing is wasted. Death and decay fuel new life. The carbon dioxide we exhale and the oxygen plants produce are by-products for one and essential products for the other. In this situation in which nothing is wasted and nothing is lost, we find an all-win example of symbiosis.

We would like to extend this all-win, life-enhancing principle of symbiosis to C4 communities as we consider the social architecture needed to design and create them. In so doing, we unavoidably enhance the meaning of *symbiosis* beyond the scientific definition that focuses only on physical relationships. In our definition, we include mutually beneficial relationships in the mental, relational, and spiritual realms of human and soul experience. In C4 communities, we need to consider the full potential of all the members.

In the 1800s, a religious sect known as the Shakers flourished in the United States. Their purpose was to develop an intentional community that created heaven on earth. Although their way of living in celibacy is not well-suited to modern life (the sect has dwindled to only a few members in the late twentieth century), the Shakers hold values that lend themselves to C4 communities. We can find a very tender expression of their mutual caring expressed in these lyrics to a song:

What the dew is to the flower
Gentle words are to the soul

And a blessing to the giver
And so dear to the receiver;
We should never withhold.

(*Love Is Little: A Sampling of Shaker Spirituals,* Sampler Records*)*

Bringing the level of mutual care expressed by the Shakers into communities for the mutual benefit of all life extends the concept of symbiosis to one that is an all-win situation for the entire community. The entire community profits.

Integration

Integration takes us a step beyond symbiosis. It is the process of carefully fitting all the pieces into a puzzle so that they interlock with each other to create the big picture of potential. An integration of differences helps to redefine and give new and more meaningful potential to the picture. A symphony orchestra is a good example of such integration. The skill and grace with which individual musicians combine the sounds of strings, horns, percussion, and woodwinds creates a magical moment that enthralls us all. It is the very differences in all those sounds that unite in the creation of musical masterpieces.

Whereas symbiosis describes a mutually beneficial relationship in which both parties maintain their discrete identities, integration in

our use of the word describes a sharing that encourages the creation of something new and more universal. We have mentioned one example of such integration throughout this book. It is the integration of telephone technology with computer technology to create the Internet. Neither telephones nor computers alone could feed information to a knowledge-hungry world the way the Internet does. In effect, integration honors human relationships and actual and potential relationships throughout the web of life.

Synergy

Synergy is a building process in which each success provides energy for the next success. It is the result of all-win symbiosis and creative integration of disparate elements. This synergistic building process happens in any number of situations.

A classic example of synergy occurs with winning sports teams. When team members are "in the groove," they are unstoppable. Each winning play builds the rapport among members and builds their collective energy for the next success. Players often refer to synergy as a peak team experience. When they occur, these synergistic experiences are the result of symbiosis and integration. That is, members work for their mutual benefit and integrate their skills to become a highly effective team.

Another example is urban renewal, in which an act as simple as cleaning and restoring a playground creates neighborhood pride. This pride fuels new energy to improve the appearance of the area. With a growing sense of pride in place, neighbors might then unite to reduce crime in the area to make the neighborhood safe and enjoyable. Success fuels success and creates a community's awareness of its potential.

The notion that success fuels success is essential to synergy. The result is always that the whole is greater than the sum of the parts. Synergy is, in effect, the joy emanating from successful C4 communities.

INTEGRATION IN SUMMARY

Gus and I have a friendly joke that between the two of us, I am the immanent one and he is the transcendent one. Although we kid about it, the truth of the statement is apparent in any meeting with us. I am the pragmatist; he is the idealist. Our hope is that integration of these two differences brings life and interest to our work and this book.

As the immanent coauthor, I have a compelling need to summarize, synthesize, and integrate the main themes of our work at this point. In so doing, I review themes to the present. I have arranged this synthesis in a METAMATRIX® map (Figure 13–1).

TRANSFORMATIVE GROWTH

We started our book by embracing the sanctity of all life and therefore looking to nature for models that might guide us in the creation of a healthy, life-enhancing future. In our search, we found a general peri-

		Transformative Growth	Illustrative Maps	C4 Values	Ideal Intentions
↑	**Transform**	Transforming into next higher order	Social Architecture	Compassion	Love is the only future.
	Share	Share through integration of differences	Human Learning	Collaboration	Community is the only profit.
	Repeat	Repeat multiple likenesses	Domain Mapping	Creativity	Life is the only customer.
G R O W T H	**Gather**	Gather being or idea	Human Evolution	Conscious Evolution	Evolution is the only business.

TIME ⟶

Figure 13–1 *Summary Map of Our Book*

odicity with its universal and repeatable processes and patterns that permeate nature at all levels. As electrons orbit the nucleus of an atom, the planets of our solar system revolve around our sun. Similarly, the cycles of gather, repeat, share, transform (GRST) repeat themselves in a process-pattern of evolutionary growth.

Of the many general periodic processes and patterns throughout nature, we chose the process-pattern of transformative growth, set in Gus's creation of the METAMATRIX®, as the subject of our attention. That process-pattern of GRST is a way of evolutionary growth. Everything that learns and grows enacts and reenacts that cycle of GRST. Because the cycle is such a fundamental gathering process for everybody and everything that grows and learns, we've placed transformative growth in the gathering column, the first column of Figure 13–1.

ILLUSTRATIVE MAPS

We felt that it was critical to use the METAMATRIX® in both its four-stage and its sixteen-stage forms as the basis for our thinking and design of this book. Using our process-pattern method for ourselves seems to ensure integrity for our work. The METAMATRIX® is present in both the macro- and microstructures of this book. For example, the four ideal intentions that guide the four parts follow a GRST sequence, and we use a number of METAMATRIX® maps to illustrate our points.

Each map is an application of the GRST process-pattern. We use these applications of the METAMATRIX® map to help CEOs become proficient in our thinking process. Proficiency is a characteristic of the repeating stage of the map and is appropriate for the repeating column of Figure 13–1.

These maps illustrate both the ideal and the practical themes of our work. That is, the maps embody both our philosophy and our suggested implementation process. The map of human evolution is the largest and most profound application. The use of domain mapping provides CEOs with a useful method for creating a harmonious, profitable, and healthy future. The remaining maps, human learning and social architecture, are teaching tools for Chapter 14 and Part IV. Gus describes them and completes the last column of the human evolutionary map as we move ahead.

C4 VALUES

We have characterized the CEO as valuing conscious evolution, creativity, collaboration, and compassion. We also talk, in the domain mapping chapters, about enterprises that create value through service to their customers and all life; life is the only customer. The holding of values, acting on one's values, and creating value in services are closely intertwined. The focus on values will be one of the great business thrusts of the next millennium.

Here are two examples of why I think so. Like many Americans these days, I invest in the stock market, and though I am a very small player, I became increasingly concerned about what I was investing in. With little difficulty, I learned about socially responsible mutual funds. These socially and environmentally responsible funds invest money in companies that hold high values and create value in their products and services. For example, they treat their employees with fairness and dignity, work proactively to minimize their environmental impact, and create life-enhancing products and services. Not surprisingly, these mutual funds also produce a very respectable return on investment. They are examples of profit to both the enterprise and the community.

Charles Handy (1998), in his book *Hungry Spirit*, talks about the difficulty companies are having in attracting and keeping talented young people. The problem is that these young adults want a sense of creating value and of making a contribution in addition to a paycheck. Companies that are unable to create that sense of contribution have difficulty retaining young employees.

The same need for value is playing out in the staffing of the U.S. military. Recruiting is difficult and hampered by relatively full employment. Interestingly enough, the Marines are most successful at recruiting because of their emphasis on high standards. "A few good men" is in itself a value statement that appeals to young people over the messages of the other branches of the military. The Navy, which is having the most trouble recruiting, is working on a value-based recruiting campaign to become more attractive. In a broad sense, this need for value and contribution is an indication of a rising sense of C4 community.

The intrinsic worth of values lies in their sharability. Shared values are, after all, the foundation of all sorts of communities. Thus I place our C4 values, both for the CEO to hold and for all of us to create in new intentional communities, in the share column of Figure 13–1.

IDEAL INTENTIONS

Ideal intentions transform our thinking. They provide what we call the future pull factor. Once we gain an understanding of our ideal future, we cannot help but be pulled toward it. That pull becomes a very powerful motivator.

The creation of an ideal future depends on our ability to envision it. In setting forth our ideal intentions, Gus and I have created a future-pull vision for ourselves and, we hope, for CEOs. That vision becomes a clear destination, and with that destination held as an ideal, we are ready to start our evolutionary journey. In putting our four ideal intentions of evolution, life, community, and love in the transforming column of Figure 13–1, Gus and I hope to stimulate your thinking about the ideal future humanity can create together.

SYNTHESIS IN SUMMARY

The main columns of Figure 13–1 integrate and summarize the main themes of this book. We have a further opportunity to relate and interweave these themes to create the full fabric of Gus's and my intention. To complete our synthesis of the themes, I interrelate the rows of Figure 13–1. This approach of combining the gather rows (G_g, R_g, S_g, and T_g) and repeating the process for the repeat, share, and transform rows completes the interweaving of the themes of CEO work.

Gathering Evolution

Starting with the gather row, we can see this progression: Gather being or idea, human evolution, conscious evolution, evolution is the only business.

We start with the birth of a being or idea and move to repeating that being or idea in the context of humanity. The step from gather to repeat changes the focus from individual growth and learning to the growth and learning of our species in the past, present, and future. Our opportunity for the future is the conscious evolution to purposeful health, happiness, and valuable service to and for all life. As individual CEOs, we can take responsibility for conscious evolution. Gus's and my ultimate call, however, is for enterprises of all sorts to join in the work of creating conscious evolution by embracing and acting the ideal intention that evolution is the only business.

Repeating Creative Life

Moving to the repeat row, we see the dynamic is that multiple likenesses find expression in this progression: Repeat multiple likenesses, domain mapping, creativity, life is the only customer.

Domain mapping is a method for the repetition of multiple likenesses because it is designed to help CEOs create many successful endeavors across all domains. Those domains include the work of for-profit and nonprofit enterprises. Because domain mapping is based on the GRST sequence of evolutionary growth, we offer it to call forth the idea that the business of business is evolution. Gus has designed domain mapping to enhance the creativity of those who use it and to underscore our ideal intention that life is the only customer.

Sharing C4 community

In the share row, the progression focuses on integration: Share through integration of differences, human learning, collaboration, community is the only profit.

Guided by the dynamic of the integration of differences, we introduce the concept that human learning and collaboration are two keys in the creation of C4 community. The significance of the human learning map, which Gus describes in the next chapter, is that what and how we learn as human beings contributes to our sense of collaboration and our willingness to embrace the ideal intention that community is the only profit.

Transforming Compassion into Love

Last we find ourselves in the transform row: Transforming into next higher order, converging maps and social architecture, compassion, love is the only future.

The top row is the place of true evolutionary challenge and opportunity. Transformation, as Gus explains, is the time for asking questions about what might be. This row is the source of Gus's and my vision of the future, a time of transformation to the next higher order of being for humanity.

In Chapter 14, Gus looks at the convergence of the maps of human evolution and human learning guided by the principles of social architecture. That part is where we envision the transformation of compassion into our ideal intention that love is the only future.

FAREWELL

Because this is my last chapter, I want to wish you farewell. I hope that you have enjoyed our journey as much as I have. The final two chapters of our book are in the realm of Gus's expertise. He guides us as CEOs through the ideal intention of community as the only profit and into love as the only future.

If you have enjoyed our work together, Gus and I would like to keep the conversation with you going. We invite you to contact us at

Social Architect Associates
P.O. Box 337
Thetford Center, VT 05075 U.S.A.

or on the Internet at: Susan.B.Gault@valley.net

Best regards and a sincere wish for your joyful and healthy evolutionary future.

14

Call for a New Story of the Cosmos

I believe the future is so much a matter of the awakening soul and spirit of all humans that doing the business of evolution as chief evolutionary officers (CEOs) and social architects requires our searching and listening deeply to our own hearts. "We have evolved as far as intellect will take us," says Gary Zukav (1989) in *The Seat of the Soul*. The era of evolution requires of us profound wisdom, which means thinking with our hearts. This is a call not to abandon reason but to evolve with it into even higher capabilities of human knowing that draw from the infinite wisdom of the universe. I believe that the heart has its reasons which reason cannot know. Our souls have intentions and contracts to fulfill way beyond the machinations of our personalities and our intellects.

To assist our focus on community building, this chapter offers new thinking perspectives to help you in considering how to create conscious, creative, collaborative, compassionate (C4) community. We discuss C4 values and call for cosmological thinking. We provide a new map of the practice of social architecture as we present it in this book. And we introduce a map of human learning, which provides a broad picture of the learning stages that support creation of C4 community.

COSMOLOGY: CREATING OUR OWN STORY

Casting the broadest net of meaning possible as CEOs and social architects, we owe ourselves a beginning search for a personal cosmology to share and unite with others. A cosmology is a story of how and why the universe exists. In some ways, it is the largest thinking, planning, and design tool humanity has. In the emerging renaissance of conscious evolution, which we are helping to define, there is a great need to find a grand, unified story that can integrate and synthesize the human knowings of the physical, mental, emotional, soulful, and spiritual aspects of our human being and of the universe.

This search is a tall order, but we are making a beginning now as we return to the definition of social architecture and to the four Cs of ideal intentional community. The enactment of these values in community is the inspiration for the ideal intention that community is the only profit.

CONSCIOUS COSMOLOGY

The four Cs have not only social but also cosmological importance for us. To begin with the first C, the word *conscious*, we are evermore aware that consciousness is causal. That is, what we think is what we get. Our thoughts become our material and nonmaterial reality. At the cosmological level, our stories are continuously evolving, for example, from the action-reaction physics of Newton to the relativity of Einstein to our current quantum mechanics. What we hypothesize, validate, and project, the universe embraces, confirms, and returns to us.

Is there a cosmological story now evolving that will embrace and include the human mind and heart, the soul and spirit? Humanity can no longer endure leaving these elements of our lives and our world out of our story. Our cosmological story has been unbalanced on the side of the physical and the material, and it has been almost the sole property of physics and related sciences. This unbalance is one of the causes of the excesses of our materialistic culture. It is now time to project all of ourselves, the fullest and deepest meanings of our humanity, into the universe to create our cosmological renaissance story. CEOs are flying blindly without their own universe story. With our own universe story, as with the creation of community, we gain integrity and synergy when the C4 values are common to both community and cosmology.

The cosmos has given us order for free. It is our purpose and privilege as CEO social architects to learn to collaborate in building with the gifts of divine grace revealed in natural order.

CREATIVE COSMOLOGY

Creative is the second C in the values of new ideal community and cosmology. All our creations are experienced first as ideas that are like miniature reenactments of the "big bang" creation of the universe. Our thoughts burst forth to become the inspirational light and the electrical stimulation to action in our bodies. Remembering that our creativity is indeed a universal act can help us reorient our intentions toward bringing forth the greatest good for the most beings, toward a story and a business of conscious evolution.

COLLABORATIVE COSMOLOGY

Collaboration, the third C, is conscious creative cooperation that causes highly synergetic outcomes way beyond the sum of the parts and the sum of the participants. This natural ephemeralization that creates more ability and goodness with less effort, like geese flying in formation, is another key to and proof of the profit of community. Doing more with less puts us in a more fair and balanced position with the planet's bounteous gifts and in a more generous and sharing mode with all life.

COMPASSIONATE COSMOLOGY

The last C is *compassion*, which is acting from a loving heart and feeling that love for others. Compassion frames the four Cs in an orientation whereby community design can be cosmological in scope and soul and spirit centered. We have said that the meaning we project into the universe is returned to us. Compassion, a loving heart, is one of the greatest gifts we can give to our C4 cosmology and community.

SOCIAL ARCHITECTURE OF C4 COMMUNITY

A fundamental purpose of social architecture is to create C4 community. The definition of social architecture is a call and guide to us. I offer this definition again for inspiration about the depths of assistance available to us as social architects. We become workers for the evolving universe and its beneficence when we consider the following words: Social architecture is divine grace revealed in natural order used for the planning and enhancement of human fulfillment.

I believe that divine grace, as the opening concept, places us in a cosmos created by a source whose nature is compassionate support, or more broadly, infinite and unconditional love. Divine grace tells us that the wisdom of the universe is teaching us to think with our hearts and to see and receive that grace. Divine grace revealed in natural order tells us that nature and all its exquisite order is a revelation of grace. Nature is the architecture of love.

Nature is not just blood red in tooth and claw to be fought against and defended against. Even in the predatory food chain in which we are all enmeshed there is a beautiful balance and harmony when and if we see, feel, and express the blessing and sanctity in life feeding life. Food, when held in reverence, acknowledges the holiness of life. The saying of grace at mealtime is one way we acknowledge the divine grace of natural order given us.

The phrase *used for the planning and enhancement* is perhaps the closest to our common conception of the work of an architect. We think of great architecture as the embodiment of noble ideals with wonderfully functional form, flow, and focus for enhanced living. Yet here the

definition of social architecture moves away from physical building to a focal purpose: planning and enhancement of human fulfillment. Human fulfillment says that in the realms of grace and order there is yet a higher and further place for humanity to evolve. Humans have a destiny of fulfillment as yet unknown. In the unfolding of cosmic order, which we are always seeking out and reflecting on with wonderful curiosity and yearning, there is more for us.

What is the human fulfillment that our evolving natural order has in store for us? As a partial answer and as help in the design process for you, the social architect of conscious evolution, we have offered a third new column of suggested concepts in the macrostory of human evolution in Chapter 12. We also have two new maps to offer. The first shows our work so far together as social architects. The second is a map of human learning. Not surprisingly, they begin to merge and integrate.

MAP OF SOCIAL ARCHITECTURE

Let us take a look at a map of our work together as social architects, shown in Figure 14–1 in which the third sharing column is the same as our suggested sharing column in the map of human evolution. We presume that this unification would serve as a guide to any social architecture design initiatives. The map proceeds from conscious evolution to creative life to collaborative community and then to compassionate love.

Conscious Evolution

The social architecture map begins with an interest in searching for patterns of deep structure and process in nature. Referring to Leonardo da Vinci and Bucky Fuller and Margaret Mead, we have said that such interest is a hallmark of renaissance and evolutionary thinkers and designers. Next we have told our story of the discovery of a repeating pattern of general periodicity in the stages of transformative growth. And we presented the creation of a generic open map called the METAMATRIX® to apply that natural order repeatedly to any and all subjects of growth and evolution that concern us.

	Conscious Evolution	Creative Life	Collaborative Community	Compassionate Love
Transform	T Map of Human Evolution	Evolutionary creativity	Transform values into peace and health in all relations	T_t
Share	Domain Mapping Application	Community creativity	Share global C4 value news	T_s
Repeat	METAMATRIX	Group creativity	Create C4 communities and values in all contexts	T_r
Gather	Deep structure in nature	Individual creativity	Pioneer C4 communities and values	T_g

G R O W T H ↑ (vertical axis)

TIME →

Figure 14-1   *Map of Social Architecture*

To share that process, Sue has written several chapters to teach us how to apply the METAMATRIX® to mapping the domains of our endeavors. Such mapping is aimed at helping CEOs evolve their domains in a way that serves all life.

In the gathering stage of our search for a way to begin conscious evolution work as CEOs and social architects, we have presented a map of human evolution. This map serves as an image of the transformative nature of human evolution and tells the story of our recently ever more rapid evolutionary acceleration.

Creative Life

The second column of the map of social architecture focuses on the progression of who is doing the repeatable work inspired by the call of life to evolve. Individual CEOs are the first to answer. They then form groups of creative colleagues. They put the agenda of conscious evolution into the mode of C4 thinking together. Next is the creation of intentional C4 communities hosted by the groups of CEO social architects. We suggest in the transformative stage of that column (R_t) that whatever their form, intentional communities are where the best potential for evolutionary creativity and design can occur. They are where C4 community and cosmological values can and will evolve. That work is truly transformative, evolutionary creativity.

Collaborative Community

Designing for the highly synergetic outcome of the sharing dynamic requires a combination of three ideals: ideal context, relations, and values. We begin focusing the share column of the map of human evolution on the creation of pioneer C4 communities and values. That is also the focus of our work as social architects. That is, our individual life work can evolve the life of the species far more than we might imagine. The example of the worldwide influence of the Findhorn community in Scotland is a case in point; many individuals who have lived there are now formidable CEOs.

In Figure 12–1 we give examples of the human-evolution sharing column titled All-life Relations with descriptions of imagined scenarios. Also in Chapter 12, I define pioneer C4 community with the Abode Community as another example of pioneering living. In Chapter 15, I look farther to the future and to C4 community as the embodiment of a new, unified cosmological orientation.

MAP OF HUMAN LEARNING

The next design element is a map of human learning. CEOs as social architects are working at a time when human learning, accelerating in rate and scope, is a powerful evolutionary force in business, science, education and all other domains. It is essential that CEOs seeking to analyze and plan learning strategies have a developmental map of human learning. A CEO needs epistemological orientation, a notion of the sequence of the stages of learning as individual lives progress and mature and as the human species evolves. Such an orientation is a vital element of our social architecture. It helps us consciously evolve how we learn and what we need to know in any of our evolutionary initiatives and endeavors. Remembering Gary Zukav's (1989) saying, "We have evolved as far as intellect will take us," we now need to collaboratively open up our innate higher ways of knowing to consciously evolve. So we are offering a preliminary first sketch of a map that we hope you will continue to develop yourself.

The logic in this thinking map is, of course, our understanding of the third-stage dynamics of sharing: the beneficial synthesis and integration of differences as in sex, creed, race, or nation. An example is the combining of wide diversity into higher-order unity, as in the American melting pot phenomenon of multicultural creativity, *e pluribus unum*, from the many one. Other examples include the continuous need for the creative resolution of personal freedom and the public good and the critical need for a higher-order unity of the world environment and the world economy. These, like the simple power of metaphor in Homer's line "the ships plowed the sea," all achieve a union of creativity and synergistic potential far beyond addition and even multiplication of their elements.

The sharing dynamic is the central mode of being in the next macro stage of human cultural and social evolution. We should find that any consideration of human individual and species behavior evolving into higher states of fulfillment would also build on the sharing dynamic. That building is the case we find in our formulation of a map of human learning, a map of how we evolve in thinking and learning and knowing what we know.

Our work in making this map is based on the idea of the evolving stages of human development suggested by other developmental theorists such as Piaget, Maslow, Erikson, Gowan, Kohlberg, and Gilligan. Our model is rough and simple. It is a beginning sketch of our human potential for the future. As Sue has said with blunt humor, all models are wrong, some are useful. So in offering this learning map as a design element for your consideration as a social architect and planner of human fulfillment, we hope this sketch opens up an area of thinking for you in a useful way.

The map of our evolution as human learners (Figure 14–2), follows the gathering, repeating, sharing, and transforming sequence

		Information	Knowledge	Wisdom	Enlightenment
Transform	Make self-conscious meaning	Gain overview insight	Experience revelation and unititive consciousness	T_t
Share	Acquire contextual information	Gain understanding of principle	Share transcultural world wisdom	T_s
Repeat	Acquire verbal language	Acquire general knowledge	Develop transpersonal intuition and soulful community	T_r
Gather	Gather sensory data	Acquire factual knowledge	Develop intuition and whole-being knowing	T_g

(Vertical axis labeled: GROWTH, upward arrow. Horizontal axis labeled: TIME, rightward arrow.)

Figure 14–2 *Map of Human Learning*

with the four main columns progressing from information to knowledge to wisdom to enlightenment.

Information

The gathering column of information begins with the sensory data of the infant and progresses to the young child acquiring verbal repeatable language. The next stage is later childhood wherein the acquiring and sharing of contextual information, as in family and school life, is the focus of learning. In the transformation of transitory information during adolescence, the challenge is the need to make self-conscious meaning that is in resonance with and that integrates oneself with the broader culture. This cultural placement necessitates leaving off the personal, often private, world of childhood in place of learning the factual knowledge of repeatable ideas on which one's culture and society are constructed.

Knowledge

Knowledge is a higher-order construct than information. It is made so by its value, which renders it repeatable orally, in print, and in many other forms of presentation. This form of learning begins with acquiring factual knowledge and progresses to the learning of general knowledge, the ideas that are most often repeated to make the culture work, such as the concepts and facts of time. The sharing stage of knowledge calls for the learning of principles on which whole fields of knowledge are integrated.

The principles of the periodic table of elements built the science of chemistry, and the principles of transformative growth and development underlie the map we are now learning. In the realm of factual knowledge, we come to its transformation in the currently evolving, overarching theories that gain tremendous overview insight, such as general systems theory, complexity theory, and grand unification theory. They are the current upper limits to our ability to reason with knowledge and our intellects.

Wisdom

Wisdom is the sharing stage of evolutionary learning and knowing. It begins with opening up to intuition, which is a sense beyond the five physical senses, to receive knowing from our higher self, our whole being, including our soul and other nonmanifest spiritual guides. It is our whole-being intuitive knowing that often relates to spiritual guidance to help us fulfill our soul's purpose and deepen our connection to the presence of divine grace.

Intuition is the beginning of our direct connection to the wisdom of the universe. Intuition is the beginning of listening and hearing with our heart. Intuitive insights and knowing are inspired gifts of vision and feeling from which many of the creations of science, mathematics, the arts, and all realms of human endeavor evolve. The sequence usually is instantaneous intuitive total knowing followed by often long, arduous intellectual reasoning, physical work, or both to reestablish and translate the gift.

The place of the soul is central in the intuitive, evolving world of wisdom. The soul is our eternal being that lives on in timelessness. It is the carrier of our personal evolutionary promise and gift to life and the universe. That personal gift to life is our special piece of business in the evolution of humanity and earth. We cannot be in the business of evolution in a healthy way for all life without the guidance of our souls.

If an intentional community or group of people has the intuitive, soulful learning central to their purpose, they will develop together intuition beyond the personal; they will achieve the transpersonal. The community will be soul-centered and will enhance the fulfillment of each of its members' soul gifts to the evolution of life. This kind of community or group is beginning to learn the business of evolution. Intellectual concepts are not enough to create successful conscious evolution. However, the C4 planning and enhancement of human soul fulfillment may be a start.

As communities, businesses, and other groups of intuitive and soul-centered humans emerge, increase, and weave their values and experience together and share and integrate their wisdom, wisdom itself evolves. Transpersonal wisdom becomes transcultural. It finds its way to all the eternal values that are self-evident and unarguable in all cultures on the planet. Truth, respect, honesty, and compassion in relations and the contexts of life, family, and nature all are among the core values held by all humans. They are transcultural, independent of place, and common to all. They become a new and ancient currency for all humanity.

When we come to the transformation stage of world wisdom, we begin to release the need for C4 community planetary sharing and integration of our differences. Our unity of ideal intentions, globally integrated in countless ways in myriad communities, has made clear that community, based on eternal values, is the only profit. We have achieved peace and health in all our relations throughout the web of life. We have learned to integrate all such differences as the environment and the economy into higher-order harmony.

In transformation, learning evolves beyond the focus on the soul into the realm of the spirit. Although the human spirit is part of the spirit of the universe, entering these realms alone or together is less a matter of doing anything than of being the recipient of the spirit of divine grace. We often know this state of grace as given to us in revelations, signs, and, as in meditation, in moments of unitive consciousness in which we can feel all there is woven into one seamless knowing and being. We cannot command spirit but we can work to open our hearts and trust. Then spirit works though us. Such grace is pure gift from the universe.

We have just looked at the first three columns on our map of human learning. As with the maps of human evolution and social architecture, we explore the fourth column of this map in Chapter 15, where the three maps merge and synthesize into one.

INDIVIDUALS AND SPECIES AS RECIPROCAL LEARNERS

Both human individuals and the human species are of necessity special cases of one larger pattern. Any METAMATRIX® mapping of the learning stages of the human individual must be isomorphic, identical in some way of structure and process, to the learning stages of the human species and vice versa. The *vice versa* means that they are reciprocally causal. The individual and the species each cause the other to evolve.

A life, such as Christ's, can help evolve the species, and the species in its transpersonal and transcultural wisdom can evolve its individual members. Our evolution is best served when we give that wisdom to our youth earlier and they retain the youthful suppleness of creative spirit long into their old age. We hope you will use our rough sketch of a learning map to begin your own search into human learning. What you find will inform your ideas about human fulfillment and help guide your initiatives and learning designs as social architects.

By now at least, we have established the notion that human fulfillment is a developmental story and that most of the METAMATRIX® mapping stages of our mutual learning lie ahead of us. That is another source of creative excitement that is especially true because the realms of human intuition, soul, and spirit are all reaching into and coming from the realm of timeless eternal time; their nature is instantaneity. Given the slow, rolling time in the millions of years of human evolution, the coming human species evolutionary transformation, guided by soul and spirit, is truly potential in the biblical terms of the twinkling of an eye.

The powerful transformation of spiritual enlightenment and fulfillment individually and culturally is the next and final stage of human evolution on our map. It is the final macrostate in this book wherein our ideal intention is that love is the only future. Through the dynamics of transformation, we know that any final transformation stage is also the beginning stage of a whole new cycle of human evolution into new forms of grace, order, and service to life in the cosmos.

Part IV

Love Is the Only Future

Teilhard de Chardin prophesied that the day would come when humanity would discover, after harnessing all kinds of energy, that love is the primal energy. In learning to work with and become conscious love, we would have discovered fire for the second time in the history of the world. That day is now. We are learning that a new story emerging on the birth of the universe posits that the intention, source, and substance of the cosmos are the intention, idea, and energy of love.

We seek now to learn with you that for the creation of conscious evolution, any behavior other than love is so shortsighted and expensive as to be harmful for all concerned. It is time to create compassionate communities, soul circles in which to join with the divine grace of the cosmos in manifesting the behavior wherein the business of business is love and love is the only future.

15

The Higher-Order Unity of Love

In this chapter I reach farther into the realm of human spiritual knowing and being. I firmly believe that the spiritual gifts we all have, though often hidden from us in our souls, are becoming the revealed nature of our work in the world. That trend will only increase because it is the next developmental stage and natural evolutionary emergence of what it is to become more fully human. Although these next words are the ending of our book, for us and I hope for you, they are the beginning of a new era of conscious evolution wherein we also begin to explore our final ideal intention that love is the only future.

Part IV is about transformation, the transformation of each of us and of the whole human species. Transformation is about unfolding from within a whole new identity, a higher-order unity of unforeseen elevated potential. It is the stage in which the caterpillar transforms and becomes the butterfly. It is when human and humanity transform to become cosmic cocreators with the divine grace and ideal intention of the universe, which, I suggest, is cocreating with love.

We begin an exploration into how love may provide a higher-order identity and unity sufficient for all our contemporary needs for future successful evolution. We began the book with the ideal intention that evolution is the only business. We now start to glimpse a higher-order unity whereby the evolution of business and the business of evolution begin to merge into one ideal and endeavor. The business of conscious evolution calls for a higher-order unity of everything from intentional cosmology to intentional community to intentional conscious soul purpose.

Only the infinite reach and primordial universal power of love may offer us a cosmological story of grand unification capable of uniting our thinking and guiding our behavior into higher-order planetary unity. Love is more than a human emotion. Love is the creative source of the universe, the substance of all matter in the universe, and the future awakening of conscious evolution of the universe. I believe that the story of evolution proceeds from love to light to matter to life to consciousness to conscious evolution and returns to love. This is why I say that love is the only future.

CONVERGENCE IN TRANSFORMATION

This ideal intention leads us to the fourth and final transformation column on our map of human evolution. Here we achieve a higher-order unity with our maps because our suggested terms of transformation are the same on each of the three maps. Human evolution, human learning, and social architecture converge. They become one and the same map in their Transform columns, as shown in Figures 15–1 through 15–3. How we evolve as individuals and as a species is the same as how and what we need to learn singly and together. Both of these are the same as what a chief evolutionary officer (CEO) and social architect would intend, enhance, and seek to fulfill in self and others. This kind of higher unity of ideal intention is possible and desperately needed for the transformation of human evolutionary fulfillment in compassionate relations with the planet earth.

The titles on top of the three transform (T) columns of the maps in Figures 15–1 through 15–3 are all one outcome. Universal love, awakening to enlightenment, and compassionate love all are cut from the same spiritual cloth. I suggest that they are all higher forms of human knowing and being that we each have within us. They are part of our full spiritual inheritance that will emerge to shape the direction of our human evolution.

The titles of the transform columns on the maps show that the terms are the simplest of mere suggestions. Yet there is a profound difference from any of the terms in the previous columns, such as the

		Independent Nations	Collaborative Alliances	All-Life Relations	Universal Love
	Transform	Dark ages	Create conscious renaissance	Transform values into peace and health in all relations	Entering into cosmic consciousness
	Share	City-states	Information age	Share global C4 value news	Sharing the sanctity of universal wisdom
	Repeat	Agriculture	Industrial age	Create C4 communities and values in all contexts	Receiving the blessings of universal wisdom
G R O W T H	Gather	Hunter-gatherer	Renaissance: science and reason	Pioneer C4 communities and values	Opening to universal wisdom

TIME ⟶

Figure 15–1 *Four-Column Map of Human Evolution*

sharing work that we must consciously do in a C4 way in creating ideal community profit. We can consciously share, but transformation is done for us and through us from within and beyond us. The wisdom of the universe in its primordial love guides us and acts through us to fulfill our self-discovery, unfolding, and grace.

This kind of inspired and guided living and being is a higher form of human being. It is often exemplified in transcendent moments, revelations, and breakthroughs in the lives of scientists, artists, inventors, mystics, poets, and all other creative seekers. Yet it is common to all humans and will increasingly become part of our species' future evolving. Part of the art of spiritual opening depends not on adding new behaviors but on subtracting as much as possible to become open to spiritual awareness and guidance. That is why the transforming-gather (T_g) words on our three-in-one map are "Opening to universal

		Information	Knowledge	Wisdom	Enlightenment
	Transform	Make self-conscious meaning	Gain overview insight	Experience revelation and unititive consciousness	Entering into cosmic consciousness
	Share	Acquire contextual information	Gain understanding of principle	Share transcultural world wisdom	Sharing the sanctity of universal wisdom
	Repeat	Acquire verbal language	Acquire general knowledge	Develop transpersonal intuition and soulful community	Receiving the blessings of universal wisdom
	Gather	Gather sensory data	Acquire factual knowledge	Develop intuition and whole being knowing	Opening to universal wisdom

G
R
O
W
T
H

TIME

Figure 15–2   *Four-Column Map of Human Learning*

wisdom." By opening our minds, hearts, and souls, we are able to gather the grace of transformation, which is also the beginning stage of a new renaissance of successful human and planetary evolution.

The transforming-repeat (T_r) is repeatedly receiving the blessings of universal wisdom. Once the C4 relationship is open with the universe, we are advised to ask and it shall be given to us. Then at transforming-share (T_s), sharing the sanctity, the holiness of universal wisdom, and divine grace is a way to fulfill all the journeys of our souls, each in its unique way.

For the transforming-transform (T_t) stage on our maps, I suggest that while all these openings, receivings, and sharings can and will happen for us and our species over lifetimes and future ages of time, they will also happen in the timeless twinkling of an eye. Entering into this state of loving grace is entering into enlightenment or cosmic con-

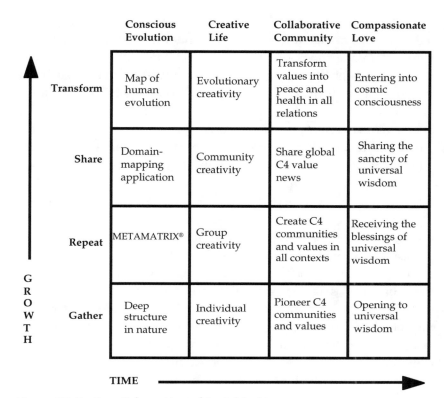

	Conscious Evolution	Creative Life	Collaborative Community	Compassionate Love
Transform	Map of human evolution	Evolutionary creativity	Transform values into peace and health in all relations	Entering into cosmic consciousness
Share	Domain-mapping application	Community creativity	Share global C4 value news	Sharing the sanctity of universal wisdom
Repeat	METAMATRIX®	Group creativity	Create C4 communities and values in all contexts	Receiving the blessings of universal wisdom
Gather	Deep structure in nature	Individual creativity	Pioneer C4 communities and values	Opening to universal wisdom

GROWTH

TIME

Figure 15–3 *Four-Column Map of Social Architecture*

sciousness. That is a state of oneness with all that is, of union with the divine being and intent of the cosmos. From that state of transformed fulfillment as humans and humanity, we may evolve to a higher order and begin the evolutionary business of expanding divine grace and love among ourselves and all planetary life and exporting grace and love out into the universe.

Expanding grace and love seems a far cry from our current notions of business expansion and exportation. Remember, however, that our species is guided in evolution by the lives of our great spiritual leaders, such as Christ and Buddha and more recent holy ones such as Mother Teresa. They are magnetic evolutionary forces for just such maturation and fulfillment of the human species. Their lives are clearly about the power of love as it expands its force and influence for evolving human health, meaning, and being.

Our current notions of business and trade are a fertile garden for rethinking the human future. It has been our experience that doing the work of thinking and beginning to feel what it might be like to live and work in the T-column transformation era of human evolution stretches us in a most healthy way. When we return to our regular daily endeavors, we see new possibilities from a totally new perspective. This kind of imaginative idealism makes it possible to plan for new creative initiatives and relationships and to enact them with more ease and certainty because we have spent time considering the highest ideals we could imagine and for which we could reach.

Because the ever-increasing power of global business is arguably the greatest planetary force of combined human creativity with the greatest potential for successfully weaving the web of peaceful human unification, what synthesizing focus for business might we imagine? Starting with Chapter 1, we suggest three sets of dynamics and values: the four GRST stages of general periodic transformative evolution (gather, repeat, share, transform), the four Cs of evolutionary community building (conscious evolution, creativity, collaboration, compassion), and the four ideal intentions (the "onlys" of evolution, life, community, and love). How might these dynamics and value sets combine into a transformative higher-order unity and identity?

CALL FOR THE COSMOLOGY OF LOVE

To pull all this thinking together into a final consideration for CEOs, I suggest that we focus our imaginations on a business dedicated to creation of the largest working tool and guiding story that the planetary culture can have and now sorely needs: a new cosmology. A new cosmology is a new grand unification story of how and why we are now in conscious cocreative business partnership with the evolution of the cosmos.

Let's imagine that all CEOs can collaborate with humanity worldwide to formulate an overarching story of the why and whereto of human evolution and our place in the universe. This C4 story telling is part of the soul work of all contemporary humans and our species as a whole. The story of the relativity of space, time, energy, matter, and light and the story of quantum mechanics, however powerful and useful, do not speak to the hearts and souls of all humans. As a species, we are almost totally disconnected from our current cosmological stories. This alienation has gone on for so long that we accept it and perhaps have been numbed by it into silence.

Imagine that every living human, all of us together, could find soul-fulfilling agreement on a hugely energizing, powerful, and totally engaging mutual creative endeavor. Imagine that we could tell each other an infinitely evolving and diverse story of how each of our lives is a gift of grace from and to the whole glorious and eternal purpose of the universe. Then we would all be about the business of divinity, of evolution, and of the universe. This cosmological story has been within us all along waiting to emerge.

Love is the only focus and force in every human life so deeply sought and felt that, as we seek the air we breathe and the water we drink, we are constantly seeking its fulfillment consciously or unconsciously. Yet all around us there are lives painfully struggling with the absence of love. Imagine the power of healing we could bring to those lives and the peace and joy we could feel with all life if we as CEOs sought to establish a cosmology of love. Imagine an evolving story wherein we daily learn to be validated by the cosmos and learn that everything within the cosmos from the start was, is now, and forever will be made by love, of love, and for love. Imagine the joy and pride of purpose within us and among us if living our lives as part of the cosmic love story and passing it on to others were a worldwide shared agreement on how and why to be human and what the universe hopes from us.

The giving and getting process in a world inspired and guided by love would have a much enriched and elegantly more simple dynamic of exchange. In an economic exchange system with the medium of money involved, we have "either-or" exchange. Either I exchange my money for your goods and services or I cannot buy them. If I buy, I have less money and more of what I bought. In the information and knowledge era, we have evolved into an often very different exchange system of "and-and" exchange. If I teach or give you some knowledge and you receive it, I still have it and so do you. It is a no-loss and you-have-it-and-I-have-it exchange.

Love is even more simple and more elegant as an all-win value. With love, the joy of loving is its own reward. The more you express and give love, the more you feel love within yourself and the more you may receive from others. Love only multiplies; it is free, it is the thing everyone wants most; it can stop time and open doors in your life. Everyone gains who comes in contact with it. Its magical benefits are infinite.

We all have seen ways in which the economic money system can cause harm when either-or dynamics are heartless and harsh. In a bionomic exchange, life itself in information and sustenance is the exchange medium, so and-and relations such as symbiosis and synergy become prevalent. If we were able in our evolutionary business of establishing a love cosmology to create *amonomics*—the relations, expressions, and exchanges of love—it would undoubtedly transform its forerunners' economics and bionomics.

The business of creating a love cosmology implies taking every subject we think about and asking and living the question, What happens if we put love at the core of this subject? If we remove today's core dynamics, such as energy, money, or success, and replace them with the understanding that love is the central formative and guiding dynamic and all else derives from it, what happens? We may find that all the core concepts of our global culture are in fact derived from the primordial universal dynamics of love. We find ourselves taking the conscious evolutionary responsibility of reorienting and transforming all our institutions and endeavors around new core values that are the ancient eternal values of the cosmos.

For instance, if we take our understanding of governance and politics through four GRST stages with two, sharing and transformation, in the future, it might sound like this. The gathering mode was led by the power of the one, the chief, ruler, emperor, or king in a monocracy. In recent historic times through numerous revolutions, we have sought to evolve into the repeating model of electoral politics from the rule of the one to the rule of the people: demos, democracy, the power of the people.

The next future mode focuses on the sharing of power with life itself. We may find humans in a C4 mode with the whole community of life consciously creating a biocracy, the power of life itself to regenerate and prevail. Biocracy would be an obvious necessity living in earth orbit or on Mars, both now on the human evolution drawing board. The fact is that biocracy or some such mode of political self-governance is rapidly becoming a necessity here on "Spaceship Earth." But our chances of evolving such self-governance are in real doubt as long as relativity and quantum energy are the central concepts of our current cosmology.

When we go to the transformative stage of human self-governance and politics amid the business of creating a love cosmology, we may formulate amocracy, the power of love to people and life, and the power of people and life to love. What begins to emerge as we consider such concepts as amonomics and amocracy is that love—a central and critical dynamic of our human body, mind, heart, soul, and spirit—is all-pervasive and all-sufficient to any survival need and any challenge of meaning that we can face.

There are four main branches of philosophic study: the nature of being, the nature of knowing, the nature of valuing, and the nature of believing. I can think of no other aspect of our deepest felt and best known reality than love that so fully and profoundly fills the role of fundamental energy, idea, value, and belief for each of these branches of philosophy.

Love fills all four aspects of philosophy. Love is so fundamental that in one of its aspects, it is the highest form of energy from which all light, energy, and matter are made. Love is the highest and fullest idea of order from which the universe and all its actions, from the spin of an electron to the spin of a galaxy, derive. Every human idea is a fractal part of the idea of universal order that is love. Love is the ultimate value as the relation that holds the universe of being together in connective, harmonious integrity. Love is the unitive power and presence common to all religious and spiritual beliefs that gives them their deepest potential to heal, nurture, and to glorify with joy the human soul and spirit.

Love is resonance and reverence with the energy, idea, feeling, value, and spirit of the universe. It is living in grand unification with the cosmos; it is being the cosmological story of divine grace. Love is the ideal focus and intention for the business of conscious cosmology and conscious evolution created and guided by CEOs with the soul-fulfilling participation of all humans.

Here is one last story about why we say that love is the only future. It is a small gift from me to you in your noble effort to become a CEO.

In 1987 during a conference I was hosting in Florence, I visited Assisi. I arrived in a state of exhaustion and pain and went to a hotel and darkened my room. I prayed to Saint Francis for guidance about social architecture and cosmology. Just before sleeping, I wrote in the dark. These are some of the words I read when I awoke:

Love is infinite in experience and meaning.

How could it not be; it is the source, substance and future of all being.

So, if you would build anything, build it on a web of love and it will be both ephemeral and timeless, momentary and enduring.

Bibliography

Ainsworth-Land, George T. *Grow or Die*. New York: John Wiley and Sons, 1986.

Anderson, Ray O. *Midcourse Correction*. White River Junction, VT: Chelsea Green, 1999.

Baskin, Ken. *Corporate DNA*. Boston: Butterworth–Heinemann, 1998.

Bentov, Itzhak. *Stalking the Wild Pendulum*. Rochester, VT: Destiny Books, 1988.

Benyus , Janine M. *Biomimicry*. New York: Morrow, 1997.

Bleedorn, Berenice. *The Creativity Force in Education, Business, and Beyond*. Lakeville, MN: Galde Press, 1998.

Bruns, Roger. *Thomas Jefferson*. New York: Chelsea House Publishers, 1986.

Bucke, Richard Maurice. *Cosmic Consciousness*. New York: Carol Publishing Group, 1993.

Carter, Forrest. *The Education of Little Tree*. Albuquerque: University of New Mexico Press, 1976.

Catford, Lorna, and Michael Ray. *The Path of the Everyday Hero*. New York: Jeremy P. Tarcher, 1991.

Chawla, Sarita, and John Renesch, eds. *Learning Organizations*. Portland, OR: Productivity Press, 1995.

Clark, Kenneth. *Leonardo da Vinci.* London: Penguin Books, 1989.

Depree, Max. *Leadership Is an Art.* New York: Dell Publishing, 1989.

Doczi, Gyorgy. *The Power of Limits.* Boulder, CO: Shambala, 1981.

Edmundson, Amy. *A Fuller Explanation.* Boston: Birkhauser, 1987.

Erikson, Erik. *Identity and the Life Cycle.* New York: W.W. Norton, 1994.

Ferguson, Marilyn. *The Aquarian Conspiracy.* New York: Jeremy P. Tarcher (division of Putnam), 1980.

Fox, Matthew. *The Reinvention of Work.* HarperCollins, New York, 1995.

Fuller, R. Buckminster. *Critical Path.* New York: St. Martins Press, 1981.

Gardner, Howard. *Multiple Intelligences.* New York: BasicBooks, 1993.

Gardner, John W. *Building Community* [pamphlet]. Washington, DC: Independent Sector Leadership Studies Program, 1969.

Gaustad, Edwin S. *Sworn on the Altar of God.* Grand Rapids, MI: William B. Eerdmans, 1996.

Gilligan, Carol. *In a Different Voice.* Cambridge, MA: Harvard University Press, 1982.

Gowan, John Curtis. *Trance Art and Creativity.* Buffalo, NY: Creative Education Foundation, 1975.

Gowan, John Curtis. *Operations of Increasing Order.* Westlake Village, CA: John Curtis Gowan, 1980.

Gozdz, Kazimierz, ed. *Community Building: Renewing Spirit and Learning in Business.* San Francisco: Sterling and Stone, 1995.

Handy, Charles. *The Hungry Spirit.* New York: Broadway Books, 1998.

Hawken, Paul. *The Ecology of Commerce.* New York: HarperBusiness, 1993.

Hillman, James. *The Soul's Code.* New York: Random House, 1996.

Houston, Jean. *Godseed.* Wheaton, IL: Quest Books, 1992.

Hubbard, Barbara Marx. *Conscious Evolution: Awakening the Power of Our Social Potential.* Novato, CA: New World Library, 1998.

Jantsh, Erich. *The Self-Organizing Universe*. Oxford, UK: Pergamon Books, 1980.

Jefferson, Thomas. *Jefferson Bible*. Boston: Beacon Press, 1989.

Johnson, George. *Fire in the Mind*. New York: Alfred A. Knopf, 1995.

Jones, Laurie Beth. *Jesus CEO*. New York: Hyperion, 1995.

Judge, Anthony J.N., et al. *Encyclopedia of World Problems and Human Potential*. Union of International Associations. Munich: Saur, 1986.

Judge, Anthony J.N. *The Aesthetics of Governance . . . in the Year 2491: An Essay*. Brussels, Belgium: Union of International Associations, 1991.

Keck, L. Robert. *Sacred Eyes*. Boulder, CO: Synergy Associates, Inc., 1992.

Kohlberg, Lawrence. *Stages of Ethical Development*. New York: Harper-Collins, 1991.

Land, George, and Beth Jarman. *Breakpoint and Beyond*. New York: HarperBusiness, 1992.

Langham, Derald. *Genesa*. Fallbrook, CA: Aero Publishers, 1969.

Lappé, Frances Moore. *Diet for a Small Planet*. 20th anniv. ed. New York: Ballantine Books, 1991.

Lawlor, Robert. *Sacred Geometry*. New York: Crossroad Publishing Co, 1982.

Lewin, Roger. *Complexity*. New York: Macmillan, 1992.

Linden, Eugene. *The Future in Plain Sight*. New York: Simon and Schuster, 1998.

Lipnack, Jessica, and Jeffrey Stamps. *Age of the Network*. New York: John Wiley, 1996.

Lipnack, Jessica, and Jeffrey Stamps. *TeamNet Factor*. Essex Junction, VT: Oliver Wright, 1993.

Love Is Little: A Sampling of Shaker Spirituals. Rochester, NY: Sampler Records, 1992.

Mander, Jerry. *In the Absence of the Sacred*. San Francisco: Sierra Club Books, 1992.

Maslow, Abraham, H. *Toward a Psychology of Being*. New York: Van Nostrand Reinhold, 1968.

McHarg, Ian L. *Design with Nature*. Garden City, NY: Doubleday, 1971.

McLaughlin, Corinne, and Gordon Davidson. *Builders of the Dawn*. Shutesbury, MA: Sirius Publishing, 1986.

Moore, Thomas. *The Care of the Soul*. New York: Harper Perennial, 1992.

Murphy, Pat, and William Neil. *By Nature's Design*. San Francisco: Chronicle Books, 1993.

Needleman, Jacob. *A Sense of the Cosmos*. New York: E.P. Dutton, 1976.

Piaget, Jean, and Barbel Inhelder. *The Psychology of the Child*. New York: Basic Books, 1969.

Quinn, Daniel. *Ishmael*. New York: Bantam/Turner, 1992.

Renesch, John, ed. *New Traditions in Business*. San Francisco: Sterling and Stone, 1991.

Rifkin, Jeremy. *The Biotech Century*. New York: Jeremy P. Tarcher/Putnam, 1998.

Sanford, Charles B. *The Religious Life of Thomas Jefferson*. Charlotte: University Press of Virginia, 1984.

Senge, Peter. *The Fifth Discipline*. New York: Currency Doubleday, 1994.

Sessions, George, ed. *Deep Ecology for the 21st Century*. Boston: Shambala, 1995.

Sevens, Ramon. *Whatever Happened to Divine Grace?* Walpole, NH: Stillpoint Publishing, 1988.

Sprigg, June, and David Larkin. *Shaker Life, Work, and Art*. New York: Houghton Mifflin, 1991.

Sturner, William. *Mystic in the Marketplace*. Buffalo, NY: Creative Education, Inc., 1944.

Teilhard de Chardin, Pierre. *The Phenomenon of Man*. New York, Harper and Row, 1959.

Tobias, Michael, and Georginanne Cowan, eds. *The Soul of Nature*. New York: Penguin Books, 1996.

Twyman, James F. *Emissary of Light*. Santa Rosa, CA: Aslan Publishing, 1996.

Wilbur, Ken. *A Brief History of Everything*. Boston: Shambala, 1996.

Wilson, E.O., ed. *Biodiversity*. Washington, DC: National Academy Press, 1988.

Wilson, Edward O. *The Diversity of Life*. New York: W. W. Norton, 1992.

Zimmerman, Brenda, Curt Lindberg, and Paul Pesek. *Edgeware*. Irving, TX: VHA Inc., 1998.

Zukav, Gary. *The Seat of the Soul*. New York: Simon and Schuster, 1989.

Index

A

Abode, The, 134
acceleration of evolution, 4, 60, 64
astrophysical, 34, 36

B

biomimicry, 143–144
bionomy (world), 132
biophysical, 14, 34, 35
Bluebeard's ship, 140
business, leading evolution 70–72

C

C4 community, 9, 21, 132, 139–153
  creating, 144
  social architecture of, 157–159
  stories of, 140–144
C4 community values, 9, 46, 137, 150–151
chief evolutionary officer, 6–10
  in business, 45
  characterization of, 50–51
  as conscious evolutionary, 46
  definition of, 6
  role of, 127
  using the METAMATRIX®, 53
  values of, 46
collaboration, 47
communication era, 64
community 127–138
  Abode, The, 134
  C4, 139–153
  collaborative, 161
  definition of, 128–129
  Findhorn, 133
  as fulcrum of evolution, 133
community context, 136–137
community health insurance, 141
community is the only profit, xxi, 10, 125,
  130, 138
compassion, 48, 152,
conscious cosmology, 156

conscious evolution, 4, 51, 64, 159–160, 171
  definition of, 46
conscious renaissance, 115–123
cosmology, 155–157
  conscious, 156
  of love, 176–180
CPSI. *See* Creative Problem Solving Institute
creative life, 160–161
Creative Problem Solving Institute, 32–38
creativity, 47

D

Darwinism, 131
da Vinci, Leonardo, 11, 159
de Chardin, Teilhard, 25, 169
deep structure, 7, 12, 14, 23, 24
devolution, 4
domain map, 67–68
  gather stage, 96, 106
  generic, 93–102
  GRST stages of, 86–87
  questions in generic, 95–102
  repeat stage, 97, 108
  sample map, 103–113
  share stage, 98, 109
  transform stage, 99, 110
domain mapping, xx, 65, 83–91
  application of METAMATRIX®, 20
  creation of, 78–79
  definition of, 83
  evolutionary context for, 68–70
  food industry, 80–82, 88, 103–113
  four columns, 73
  how to do, 93–102
  in information age, 69
  in map of human evolution, 69–70
  overview of, 67–70
  predictive power of, 72–73
  purpose of, 47
  sample map, 103–113

Dymaxion World Map 27, 120
dynamics of information age, 85
dynamics of sharing, 144

E
ephemeralization, 26, 120
era of evolution, 3, 23, 151
evolution, 127–131
  acceleration of 4, 60, 64
  of evolution, 131
  lead by business, 70–72
  map of human (sharing stage), 133–138
evolution, conscious, 4, 51, 64, 159–160, 171
  definition of, 46
evolution is the only business, 1, 10, 71, 112
evolutionary, definition of, 5–6

F
fibonacci spiral, 57
Findhorn community, 133
First World Congress of the New Age, 30, 122
food industry domain mapping, 80–82, 88, 103–113
  sample domain map, 105
Ford, Henry, 50
four-column thinking in METAMATRIX®, 19
fractal, definition of, 18
fractal growth pattern, 56
fractal process in METAMATRIX®, 18
Fuller, Buckminster, 26–29, 119, 159
  as philosopher of love, 28

G
gathering stage, definition of, 16
general periodicity, 12–14, 29, 55–56
  definition of, 12
  discovery of, 23–26
  transformative growth as an example of, 14–15
general systems theory, 26
generic domain map, 93–102
  questions in, 95–102
golden mean proportion, 57
golden rectangle, 57
Gowan, John A., 34
GRST progressions, 73
GRST stages, xix, 37
  of domain map, 86–87

H
Handy Charles, 150
health insurance, community, 141
Hubbard, Barbara, 31–32, 119, 121,
human evolution, xx, 78, 5
  map of, 60–62, 112
  map of gather stage, 62–63

map of repeat stage, 63–65
map of share stage, 133–138
map of transform stage, 172–173
human learning. *See also* map of human learning
  map of gather, repeat, and share stages, 161–166
  map of transform stage, 173–174

I
ideal intentions, xx, 9–10, 25, 111, 151
  creation of, 110–113. *See also* community is the only profit; evolution is the only business; life is the only customer; love is the only future
idealism, visionary, 48
information age, dynamics of, 85
integration, 146–147
integration of differences, in community, 127
intentional community, The Abode, 134

J
Jefferson, Thomas, 11, 25, 48–49
Jesus, 25
Jarman, Beth, 34, 72
Jobs, Steve, 50

L
Land, George, 33, 72
Land Institute of Kansas, 143
learning map. *See* map of human learning
life is the only customer, xx, 10, 75, 77, 91, 112
life, web of, 129–130
love is the only future, xx, 10, 25, 169
love
  cosmology of 176–180
  unity of, 171

M
macrophysical, 14
map of human evolution, xx, 78, 112,
  as application of METAMATRIX®, 20
  map of gather stage, 62–63
  map of repeat stage, 63–65
  map of share stage, 133–138
  map of transform stage, 172–173
map of human learning, xx
  as application of METAMATRIX®, 21
  map of gather, repeat, and share stages, 161–166
  map of transform stage, 173–174
map of social architecture, xx, 159–161
  as application of METAMATRIX®, 21
  map of gather, repeat, and share stages, 159–161
  map of transform stage, 175–176
mapping individual growth, 78
Mead, Margaret, 29–31, 119, 120, 159

Mendeleyev, 12, 38
METAMATRIX®, xviii–xx, 15, 16–21, 23
  applications of, 20–21
  creation of, 53–60
  as a domain map, 78–79
  four-column thinking, 19–20
  fractal process-pattern, 17
  natural order in, 16–19
  as a thinking tool, 58
METAMATRIX® dynamics. *See*
    METAMATRIX® stages
METAMATRIX® maps
  domain map, 67–68, 86–87, 93–113
  human evolution, xx, 20, 60–64, 78, 112,
    133–138, 172–173
  human learning, xx, 21, 161–166, 173–
    174
  illustrative, 149–151
  social architecture, xx, 21, 159–161, 175–
    176
METAMATRIX® stages
  gathering, definition of, 16
  repeating, definition of, 17
  sharing, definition of, 17
  transforming, definition of, 17
microphysical, 14, 34, 35

N
National Bicentennial Celebration, 31
natural order, 7, 12, 18
  as a thinking tool, 15–16, 24
natural patterns, 11
nature, patterns and processes in, 13
Nucor Steel, 141

O
ontogeny, definition of, 79
organization in nature, 34
  chart of, 35–36

P
patterns in nature, 11, 13
periodic table of elements, 12
periodicity. *See* general periodicity
phylogeny, 79
pioneer C4 community, 134, 136
predictability, 12
  with domain mapping, 72–73
processes in nature, 13
process-pattern, xviii–xix, 7, 14, 53–54
  fractal, 18
  of the book, xx
product, definition of, 87
Public Service Company of New Hamp-
    shire, 142

R
reciprocal learners, 166–167
renaissance, conscious, 115–123

repeating stage, definition of, 17
R_t time, 115–123

S
Saint Francis of Assisi, 25, 180
sample domain map, 103
service, 103
  definition of, 88
Shaker song, 145
sharing stage
  definition of, 17
  dynamics of, 144
social architect, role of, 127
Social Architect Associates, how to con-
    tact, 153
social architecture, 118–123, 155
  of C4 community, 157–159
  definition of, 37
  map of gather, repeat, and share stages,
    159
  map of transform stage, 175–176
Society for General Systems Research
    (SGSR), 29
stages of growth, GRST, 37
stages of transformative growth, 14
symbiosis, 48, 144
SYNCON, synergistic convening, 31, 121
synergy, 147

T
Town Meeting 2000, 31, 32, 122
transformation, stage of maps, 172–176
transformative growth, 14–15, 148–149
  discovery of, 33–38
  GRST dynamics of, 8
  stages of 14, 34–37
transforming stage, definition of, 17

U
unified field theory, 34

V
value-based services, 87
values, 103
  C4, 137, 150
  of C4 community, 9
  of a CEO, 46
vision, 111
  definition of, 49
visionary leaders, examples of, 50

W
web of life, 129–130
World Future Society, 31
World Game, The, 26, 120
Wozniak, Steve, 50

Butterworth–Heinemann Business Books . . . for Transforming Business

After Atlantis: Working, Managing, and Leading in Turbulent Times
Ned Hanson, 0-7506-9884-5

The Alchemy of Fear: How to Break the Corporate Trance and Create Your Company's Successful Future
Kay Gilley, 0-7506-9909-4

Beyond Business As Usual: Practical Lessons In Accessing New Dimensions
Michael Munn, 0-7506-9926-4

Beyond Strategic Vision: Effective Corporate Action with Hoshin Planning
Michael Cowley and Ellen Domb, 0-7506-9843-8

Beyond Time Management: Business with Purpose
Robert A. Wright, 0-7506-9799-7

The Breakdown of Hierarchy: Communicating in the Evolving Workplace
Eugene Marlow and Patricia O'Connor Wilson, 0-7506-9746-6

Business and the Feminine Principle: The Untapped Resource
Carol R. Frenier, 0-7506-9829-2

Business Ecology: Giving Your Organization the Natural Edge
Joseph M. Abe, David A. Bassett, and Patricia E. Demspey, 0-7506-9955-8

Coaching: Evoking Excellence in Others
James Flaherty, 0-7506-9903-5

Choosing the Future: The Power of Strategic Thinking
Stuart Wells, 0-7506-9876-4

Conscious Capitalism: Principles for Prosperity
David A. Schwerin, 0-7506-7021-5

Corporate DNA: Learning from Life
Ken Baskin, 0-7506-9844-6

Cultivating Common Ground: Releasing the Power of Relationships at Work
Daniel S. Hanson, 0-7506-9832-2

Diversity Success Strategies
Norma Carr-Ruffino, 0-7506-7102-5

5th Generation Management, Co-creating Through Virtual Enterprising, Dynamic Teaming, and Knowledge Networking, Revised Edition
Charles M. Savage, 0-7506-9701-6

Flight of the Phoenix: Soaring to Success in the 21st Century
John Whiteside and Sandra Egli, 0-7506-9798-9

From Chaos to Coherence: Advancing Individual and Organizational Intelligence Through Inner Quality Management
Bruce Cryer and Doc Childre, 0-75067007-X

Getting a Grip on Tomorrow: Your Guide to Survival and Success in the Changed World of Work
Mike Johnson, 0-7506-9758-X

Innovation Strategy for the Knowledge Economy: The Ken Awakening
Debra M. Amidon, 0-7506-9841-1

The Hidden Intelligence: Innovation Through Intuition
Sandra Weintraub, 0-7506-9937-X

The Intelligence Advantage: Organizing for Complexity
Michael D. McMaster, 0-7506-9792-X

The Knowledge Evolution: Expanding Organizational Intelligence
Verna Allee, 0-7506-9842-X

Leadership in a Challenging World: A Sacred Journey
Barbara Shipka, 0-7506-9750-4

Leading Consciously: A Pilgrimage Toward Self-Mastery
Debashis Chatterjee, 0-7506-9864-0

Leading from the Heart: Choosing Courage over Fear in the Workplace
Kay Gilley, 0-7506-9835-7

Learning to Read the Signs: Reclaiming Pragmatism in Business
F. Byron Nahser, 0-7506-9901-9

Leveraging People and Profit: The Hard Work of Soft Management
Bernard A. Nagle and Perry Pascarella, 0-7506-9961-2

Liberating the Corporate Soul: Building A Visionary Organization
Richard Barrett, 0-7506-7071-1

A Little Knowledge Is A Dangerous Thing: Understanding Our Global Knowledge Economy
Dale Neef, 0-7506-7061-4

Marketing Plans that Work: Targeting Growth and Profitability
Malcolm H.B. McDonald and Warren J. Keegan, 0-7506-9828-4

Navigating Cross-Cultural Ethics: What Global Managers Do Right to Keep From Going Wrong
Eileen Morgan, 0-7506-9915-9

A Place to Shine: Emerging from the Shadows at Work
Daniel S. Hanson, 0-7506-9738-5

Power Partnering: A Strategy for Business Excellence in the 21st Century
Sean Gadman, 0-7506-9809-8

Putting Emotional Intelligence to Work: Successful Leadership Is More Than IQ
David Ryback, 0-7506-9956-6

Quantum Leaps: 7 Skills for Workplace ReCreation
Charlotte A. Shelton, 0-7506-7077-0

Resources for the Knowledge-Based Economy Series

    Knowledge Management and Organizational Design
    Paul S. Myers, 0-7506-9749-0

    Knowledge Management Tools
    Rudy L. Ruggles, III, 0-7506-9849-7

    Knowledge in Organizations
    Laurence Prusak, 0-7506-9718-0

    The Strategic Management of Intellectual Capital
    David A. Klein, 0-7506-9850-0

    Rise of the Knowledge Worker
    James W. Cortada, 0-7506-7058-4

    The Knowledge Economy
    Dale Neef, 0-7506-9936-1

    The Economic Impact of Knowledge
    Dale Neef, Jacquie Cefola, Anthong G. Seisfeld, 0-7506-7009-6

    Knowledge and Special Libraries
    James A. Matarazzo, and Suzanne D. Connolly, 0-7506-7084-3

    Knowledge and Strategy
    Michael Zack, 0-7506-7088-6

    Knowledge, Groupware and the Internet
    David Smith, 0-7506-7111-4

The Rhythm of Business: The Key to Building and Running Successful Companies
David Shuman, 0-7506-9991-4

Setting the PACE® in Product Development: A Guide to Product And Cycle-time Excellence
Michael E. McGrath, 0-7506-9789-X

Synchronicity: The Entrepreneur's Edge
Jessika Satori, 0-7506-9925-6

Time to Take Control: The Impact of Change on Corporate Computer Systems
Tony Johnson, 0-7506-9863-2

The Transformation of Management
Mike Davidson, 0-7506-9814-4

What Is The Emperor Wearing: Truth-Telling in Business Relationships
Laurie Weiss, 0-7506-9872-1

Who We Could Be at Work, Revised Edition
Margaret A. Lulic, 0-7506-9739-3

Working from Your Core: Personal and Corporate Wisdom in a World of Change
Sharon Seivert, 0-7506-9930-2

To purchase a copy of any Butterworth–Heinemann Business title, please visit your local bookstore or call 1-800-366-2665.

CEO Seminars
from
Social Architect Associates

October 1999, and March, May, August, and October 2000

Social Architect Associates (SAA), which provides a range of consulting services based on the METAMATRIX®, such as domain mapping, educational services, and organizational design, is offering a series of CEO seminars in 1999 and 2000. These events offer Chief Evolutionary Officers the opportunity to deepen their understanding of the principles in this book and to apply those principles to their respective enterprises. If you are interested in attending one of these events, please contact SAA through one of the methods listed below. We customize events to the interests and needs of participants and would like to know what topics you consider vital. CEO Seminars are designed to host people from diverse enterprises. We can also design on-site seminars for you.

For further information contact Gus Jaccaci at:

45 High Bluff Road
Cape Elizabeth, ME 04107

Phone: (207) 799-0072
E-mail: joannegus@msn.com